Oceans of Blessing.

Christine Dare

4 Palace Yard
Hereford HR4 9BJ
Tel 0432 359099
Fax 0432 263408

Safeway

Sailaway!

*Discovering the Holy Spirit
on a World Cruise*

Christine Darg

New Wine Press

New Wine Press
P.O. Box 17
Chichester. PO20 6RY
England

© 1989 Christine Darg

All rights reserved. No part of this publication may be reproduced, stored in a retrieval system or be transmitted in any form or by any means, electronic, mechanical, photocopying or otherwise without the prior written consent of the publisher.

Short extracts may be used for review purposes.

Scripture quotations are taken from the Revised Standard Version ©National Council of Churches of Christ in the United States of America unless otherwise indicated.

ISBN 0 947852 46 8

Typeset in Plantin by The Ikthos Studios, Jolly's Farm, Chute Forest, Andover, Hampshire.
Printed and bound in Great Britain by Anchor Press Ltd, Tiptree, Essex

Contents

To Shelley and Ray

Introduction

Sometimes Jesus instructs his followers to sell everything to give to the poor. It may therefore seem paradoxical that we should be led to sell our possessions to buy tickets for an around-the-world cruise!

Could that possibly be God?

However, I've walked with God long enough now to learn never to limit him.

There's something about travel that opens us up to spiritual discovery. When we're released from routine, we're often free to let down our guards, to take time to seek a new spiritual dimension.

It was of all places — aboard the posh luxury liner Queen Elizabeth 2 — that I received the Baptism in the Holy Spirit. Some of you may be wondering what the Holy Spirit was doing aboard the QE2. But he's been travelling the high seas ever since Jonah bought passage on a boat to run away from God, and Paul was providentially shipwrecked on Malta!

I returned back to work at my newspaper office. But, by then, I was forever smitten by the adventurous Spirit of God.

The ability to travel could be likened to the 10th gift of the Holy Spirit, because without going and without being sent, this Gospel of the Kingdom will not be preached unto all nations. The prophet Daniel predicted that in the last days knowledge and travel will increase. The truly effective evangelist is gifted with special abilities and desire to go into all the world on planes, trains, ships, camels, canoes — or whatever

— to get the job done.

This is the story of a voyage that led to the discovery of living waters.

All the incidents and conversations in this book are true. All the persons are real, but some of their names have been changed to honour their privacy.

Special thanks go to the Richmond Times-Dispatch in Virginia for granting me a leave of absence to take the voyage; to my remarkable husband, Peter, for his unending encouragement and lifelong knack for travel; to my gifted mother for her many helpful insights with the manuscript; to Rene Tucker of Pompano Beach, Florida, for her wonderful hospitality and spiritual influence prior to the cruise; and to Miri Lev and Rachel Towers of Jerusalem for their timely prayers concerning this publication.

Christine Darg
Gloucestershire, England

'. . . Water, water, everywhere,
Nor any drop to drink . . .'

The Ancient Mariner

'. . . Jesus stood up and proclaimed: "If any one thirst, let him come to me and drink. He who believes in me, as the scripture has said: 'Out of his heart shall flow rivers of living water'." Now this he said about the Spirit, which those who believed in him were to receive . . .'

John 7: 37—39

Chapter 1

Meeting the Queen

As we jostled into the ticket and emigration line, all around us stood the proud wealth of many successful and, no doubt, aggressive lifetimes. Fellow passengers were a veritable parade of affluent wardrobes and designer luggage normally reserved for the pages of *The Sunday Times Magazine*.

"Well," my husband Peter whispered playfully, "at least we have the travel bug in common."

Our financial circumstances were perhaps a little different from our travel companions. Just a month ago, three yard sales had successfully rid us of the majority of our possessions and a second car. Out had gone my collection of antique furniture, various oriental carpets and piano, my cherished automatic dishwasher, Peter's stereo equipment.

As elated buyers hauled away our things, one of my incredulous friends said she would balk at her husband if he asked her to sell everything just to invest in a three-month trip. Even though one of my specialities was interior decorating, and I inherently loved beautiful things, I felt a strange indifference. I was glad to be rid of everything.

And now, there at quayside, silhouetted in the January sun of Port Everglades, Florida, stretched the Queen Elizabeth 2. Just that morning, her decks had shed the remnants of a New York ice storm. And if it can be said that ships are personable, I could almost sense a buoyant pleasure in her countenance as she and

I anticipated a 30,000 mile voyage together.

At the initial sight of her massive black steel hull and the frosted icing of her red and white aluminium superstructure, a first-time viewer is likely to stare in awe, as if in the presence of some great celebrity.

Promoted as the greatest ship in the world, and certainly Cunard's best known luxury liner, the QE2, as she's ubiquitously called, was primed for an international event. There were to be about 1,500 passengers aboard from more than 20 countries.

Peter toted the hand luggage behind me as we stepped into Cunard's conception of a plush and perfect world: one hissed by perpetual air conditioning, lined throughout in polished woods, chrome, padded upholstery and flamboyant carpeting.

A purser greeted us and offered to lead the way to our Five Deck cabin.

"Thanks, but I can find it," said Peter, not about to forfeit hours of poring over the ship's deck plans.

Visions of cabin fever loomed as I followed him down the stairway. We had booked minimum-priced accommodations. But, unbelievably, we had been mysteriously upgraded with a roomy outside cabin with our very own porthole. And there were side-by-side berths rather than bunks. Peter quickly learned that such a cabin should have cost us an additional £750. Such an unexpected bonus eradicated any misgivings I may have had over selling my dishwasher!

We soon discovered a veritable floating city of 13 decks aboard Cunard's 963-foot flagship. In that 'city at sea' were a shopping centre including a pharmacy, as well as a bank, two libraries, laundry, nursery, 530-seat cinema, synagogue, radio station, newspaper, hair salon, gymnasium, four pools and saunas, nine bars, and for those passengers who had money to throw away after paying their fares, a casino with a slew of slot machines.

As the sun evaporated, the ship began to vibrate and silently steal away from Port Everglades with dramatic, measured slowness.

Peter ventured to the Upper Deck to secure the necessary dining reservations. Left alone momentarily, I pondered if we could enjoy the company of the same tablemates who would be facing us morning, noon and night. So I prayed about it, as I believe that nothing is left to chance for those who are guided by God. I also felt led to ask specifically for a Jewish couple.

Peter returned laughing.

"My beloved," he grinned wryly, "we've got some pretty high-powered company on board. Two couples were ahead of me in the reservations line. Each insisted their travel agents had booked individual tables for two. Well, the maitre d' had no record of either one, so he cheerfully suggested that the couples might like to sit together. There was a long, embarrassed silence while the four of them glowered and sized each other up. Then, one fellow banged his fist on the counter and demanded to see the captain!"

I chuckled, too, hoping we'd be compatible with our tablemates. But all Peter knew about them was that they were Canadians who embarked in New York. They were being grouped with us simply because we were the only two couples on the entire cruise under the age of 40.

But I didn't have time to speculate about them. It was only a few minutes before dinner, and we hadn't unpacked.

☆　☆　☆

Our Upper Deck restaurant could serve more than 700 persons. At the entrance, a groaning board of delectable cheeses and silver trays of Florida fruits confronted us. This fruit serving table was a welcoming sight that would vary with each port: papaya in South America, cantaloupe in Cape Town and pineapple in the Pacific.

Our tablemates hadn't arrived, but our two waiters greeted us with menus that had been printed just for that meal. My eyes went instinctively to the desserts.

"Fresh strawberries in January!" I blurted, a little too enthusiastically.

"Well, I'll start with the caviar, please," I said pertly to my short waiter, who introduced himself as Charlie. He was only about 5-foot-5, but stocky, with graying hair at his temples.

Oliver, the other waiter and Charlie's partner, was just the opposite in his appearance: very tall and very lanky. They reminded us a bit of Laurel and Hardy. Oliver clucked teasingly as Peter ordered nearly every course on the menu.

We unflapped the red cloth napkins with a flourish and scanned the bustling restaurant, hoping for a glimpse of the entrance of our tablemates. All we had to do was look for another young couple, since all the other passengers looked like retirement age or older.

Then they appeared, walking briskly toward us. She was glamorous and ultra-thin as a model. Her long champagne-coloured hair bounced in cascades of curls, and she wore dazzling jewellery that was obviously the real thing. He was handsome, dark-haired and bearded in a black velvet evening suit and walked in a hurried, determined gait.

They introduced themselves as Jay and Tiffany from Toronto.

Immediately, we had a connection. With the delight as if meeting old acquaintances, Peter explained that his family had emigrated from London to Toronto when he was a boy. But when Peter mentioned that he later moved to Virginia, where his father worked in tobacco, Jay suddenly bristled.

"You don't smoke, do you?"

His darting green eyes scanned the table for any trace of cigarettes.

"Oh, no," we chorused.

"Jay is a doctor and a fanatic about not smoking," Tiffany said apologetically. "He simply cannot tolerate cigarette smoke. In fact, we had to stop sitting at the table we were assigned to when we first got on in New York because Jay got into a big row with a man over a cigar."

"We don't smoke, and we don't drink," Jay volunteered tensely.

It also came out in the conversation that they were Jewish, and although they didn't keep strict kosher laws, they nevertheless held an aversion to pork.

"Oh, so do we," Peter said.

Jay lifted a surprised eyebrow.

"Yes, we've been to Israel both as tourists and as official press," I added, "and we came away with a healthy respect for Old Testament dietary laws."

"So we don't smoke, and we don't drink, and we don't like pork!" Jay remarked cheerfully.

"Well, then," Peter said with his customary finesse, "I think we'll get along just fine."

And we all breathed a sigh of relief.

Chapter 2

Crossing the Equator

God save the Queen, and all those who sail on her, is sometimes the crewman's, or passenger's, prayer.

Although the QE2 is touted as one of the safest ships afloat with her own satellite navigating equipment, it's been said superstitiously that she's jinxed.

At least twice she has escaped potential disaster.

During an unprecedented trip to Israel in 1973, the QE2 sailed within range of Egyptian submarines. Later, President Anwar Sadat disclosed that he intervened to stop one of his submarines from torpedoing the liner, which was carrying 620 Jewish celebrants for the 25th anniversary of the revived state of Israel.

The second near-disaster was when, as the prosecution later claimed in court, the Irish Republican Army plotted to blow the 67,000-ton superliner out of the water. Police raided a house in Southampton, uncovering 350 pounds of explosives. Three men were found guilty of trying to stage a notorious international publicity stunt for the IRA.

Other bomb scares and rough Atlantic crossings have created QE2 headlines. But a friend's bon voyage note under our cabin door helped to cement our assurance of a safe journey: "EXPECTING GREAT MIRACLES FROM THE VOYAGE."

And now we were in for some lighthearted pageantry. A costumed King Neptune and his raucous court were assembling at noon on the Lido Deck for the 'initiation ceremony' of crossing the equator. The pageant was to be the highlight of activities during the five days between Caracas and our next landfall — Brazil.

Hundreds of passengers crammed the deck to witness Neptune's judgement. The ship's musicians struck up 'Anchors Aweigh' as the cruise staff marched out costumed as mermaids and courtiers. Ropebound at the end of the parade were 10 swimsuited passengers — novices of the sea — accompanied by the ship's medical staff dressed in surgical gear.

To the clicks of camera shutters and howls of laughter, each of the 10 landlubbers was laid out on an 'operating table' and heavily doused with catsup and shaving cream. Suddenly, the ship's physician found himself the victim of a well-aimed push, and he was quickly followed headlong into the pool by the dentist, a nurse and hotel officer. A free-for-all ensued, and soon half a dozen fully clothed crew members found themselves laughing and spluttering in the water.

But Peter noticed that one crew member seemed lonely. He introduced himself to Sean O'Reily.

"I noticed you the other day when you were sitting on deck," Sean said to Peter. "You were reading the Bible, and I was so surprised."

Sean said he was primarily a library steward and also an officer in the Salvation Army.

But, he sighed, life on board as a believer was terribly lonely. In fact, he said he had been roughed up, not once, but twice, because he was an uncompromising Christian. Once his jaw was smashed by drunken sailors who ridiculed him for being in the Salvation Army.

Sean was Irish, about 40, with blond hair and keen blue eyes. He'd experienced much sadness as his wife had died a few years previously, leaving him childless.

So Sean went to sea.

"I'm about to wither up and die for lack of fellowship," he confided to Peter.

I had noticed Sean on the previous Sunday at the ship's Divine Service held in the movie theatre. He distributed the prayer books and collected the offering for marine charities. I had particularly noticed him during the hymn singing while the night-club pianist belted out the accompaniment on an electric organ. Sean sang with a fervency, the blood vessels straining in his neck, as if he were trying to drum up enthusiasm for the perfunctory service.

That afternoon I went to the library to introduce myself to Sean. We experienced instant rapport and soon he was regaling me with his experiences on board.

There was the time he confronted a passenger who was promoting witchcraft in sophisticated, modern lingo just as smoothly as a cosmetician sells a new lipstick.

She was an American on a Caribbean cruise. When the self-proclaimed witch crossed Sean's path, he said you could have seen the sparks fly. He flatly told her that occult activities are condemned and forbidden by the Bible. ‡ He warned her that she had been deceived and was deceiving others.

The witch was livid.

"I have power to harm you," she threatened.

Sean retorted from the New Testament, "Greater is He that is within me than he (Satan) who is in the world."

While the ship was in port, Sean went wading and was stung in his legs by the sharp spines of a sea urchin. Sean had to limp to the ship's hospital for treatment.

The witch observed this and laughed arrogantly.

"See," she leered, "I do have power over you."

(‡ *Deuteronomy 18:10—12; Leviticus 19:31; Isaiah 8:19; 47:13—14*)

But Sean refused to yield to her suggestion and realised this was a battle in which his words were coins of faith.

"You have absolutely no power over me," he asserted boldly. "No demonic power ever has dominion over a believer. What has happened to my leg is purely coincidental, and Jesus is healing me!"

The swelling and pain completely disappeared, much to the chagrin of the evil woman, who loathed Sean and his testimony.

"But," he said, regarding me sadly, "my faith is weak now because I'm so lonely. I feel like I'm about to go under."

I promised that we would be seeing him often during the cruise. Little did I know how dramatically our friendship would culminate.

Chapter 3

Brazil

The early morning heat in Salvador, or Bahia, one-time capital of Brazil, was already oppressive. Peter's knit shirt stuck to his ribs from perspiration. We walked along the waterfront of Baixa, the lower half of the old city, then several hundred feet up the mountainous back streets, steeples becoming our guides. The Portugese colonial-style buildings were white, yellow, cracked and grilled in grayish black. Smells assaulted us from open doorways, from spoiling fruits and fish markets and from kerosene burners where spicy foods were being fried on the streets by squatting women. Other straw-hatted vendors reposed on wooden crates and offered iced orange drinks to offset the stifling heat.

Lethargic pedestrians seemed to walk in slow motion because of the heat. Some cleared their throats and spewed mucous on the cobblestones. I dodged fresh spittle and eventually rubbed blisters on my feet from plodding up and down the steep streets.

Like a tattered discarded doll, an old woman was curled in a corner of a church. She lapsed into a coughing spasm, then wiped her mouth with the back of her hand.

Houseware shops were filled with repulsive statues of dogs licking the wounds of a saint, gaudy Madonnas, and cheap ceramic Jesuses.

Outside on a smudged sidewalk lay a man with repugnant wounds. His limbs were sore-encrusted stubs, and I wondered if he were a leper. I had prepared myself for such a scene in India, but didn't expect it here.

Unshuttered windows framed portraits of listless women and children staring from within the cool darkness. Young men leaned in doorways, while their radios blared hypnotic tempos that would soon crescendo in the pre-Lenten 'Carnival' fever.

What the Mardi Gras is to New Orleans, the Carnival is to Brazil. Just before Ash Wednesday, glitter-faced Brazilians pour into the streets for four frenzied days of sensual revelry and tormented dancing, their eyes as if in a trance and their arms flailing wildly. Pagan voodooism and Catholicism are blurred into a hybrid of carnality that gluts the Bahian streets like a stream, carrying wiggling-hipped innocent children in its lurid wake.

Ironically, a church bell reminded us that we were in the 'City of Churches'. There are supposedly 365 churches in Bahia, one for each day of the year. But they all seemed to be in disrepair, crumbling, inaccessible. Every time Peter suggested that we visit a church, we came up against padlocked doors barring us from the dark sanctuaries and gold altars inside.

Peter grimaced: "This church looks as if it's barricaded for a siege."

Within a few minutes we passed at least five churches, all firmly bolted.

But if the churches seemed silent and shuttered, Satan's minions were omnipresent in the occult. Open-shirted men were decked out with chain necklaces bearing both crucifixes and witchcraft symbols. Occult shops seemed to thrive like parasites in the market place near Bahia's 17th Century cathedral. Inside one of these dingy shops, the smell of cheap incense was overpowering. On the dusty shelves wooden carvings of praying hands and crude crucifixes were equally displayed next to plastic skulls, African war masks,

20

spiritist idols and defiant carvings of clenched fists.

From the cathedral square, we hailed a taxi back to the ship. As we pulled away from the curb, my last vivid picture of Bahia was a withered, barefooted man laid out on the steps of the cathedral. The man's heel looked freshly bloodied and the wretched wound would soon dry into a filthy scab. I pointed out the man to the taxi driver in hopes we could do something, but he only shrugged indifferently and stepped on the gas.

☆　☆　☆

Tonight was to be special. At sea between Bahia and Rio, we were celebrating Jay's birthday with a specially prepared menu. But before Jay and Tiffany arrived, we had a confrontation with our waiter, Charlie.

"Don't talk to me about God," Charlie smirked, clenching his fist in my face to emphasise his point. "The wife's a Jehovah's Witness. I've heard enough."

We had been open about our faith from the beginning. One lets down his guard when relaxed at sea. And after our other waiter, Oliver, had learned Peter was a seminary graduate, he often prattled about religious matters in a jocular way, so as to belie his real spiritual hunger. We had therefore felt free to share some tracts on salvation with Oliver and he had, in turn, shown them to Charlie.

Charlie pulled one of the tracts from his waiter's jacket and made a skeptical remark. When I attempted a reply, that's when he clenched his fist in my face. But it wasn't in a threatening way, as I perceived that under his rough exterior was a soul longing for love and understanding.

"A Jehovah's Witness," I said, nonplussed. "Charlie, have you ever considered the possibility that your wife is the victim of a false cult?"

Charlie's expression changed.

Peter offered thoughtfully, "Jehovah's Witnesses are zealous, there's no doubt about that, but when it comes to the deity of Jesus and the resurrection, their doctrine is sadly in error. They have taken a razor blade to the Bible and cut out many essential Scriptures."

Now Charlie pulled a picture of his children from his wallet. He looked emotional.

"Do you know my wife refuses ever to have a blood transfusion because of her religion? I told her that these children of mine were not going to be subjected to her daft beliefs." Charlie's jaw was firm.

I piped in: "The Jehovah's Witnesses have taken out of context an Old Testament prohibition about drinking blood and misapplied it to lifesaving blood transfusions. Saint Paul warned that an earmark of a cult is when they twist the Bible to their own destruction."

We told Charlie we had a booklet in our cabin that explained how the Jehovah's Witnesses deviate from historic Christianity.

Charlie was pleased. "Let me read it. I need all the ammunition I can get."

☆ ☆ ☆

Jay and Tiffany arrived for dinner late, having made a flamboyant grand entrance. Apparently Jay's cruise wardrobe included a custom-made velvet evening suit to match every colour in Tiffany's rainbow of gowns. Tonight they were co-ordinated in dark green velvet and lime chiffon.

Having completed gourmet cooking classes, Jay's birthday menu was his special choice of avocado shells filled with lobster, followed by veal medallions and truffle sauce and then crepes prepared by the major-domo on the trolley.

By now the four of us were so relaxed that we were eating off of each other's plates when we wanted to sample a new delicacy. We had great fun trying to fatten Tiffany, whose primary aim on the cruise was to gain weight. But, alas, her favourite dishes were inevitably the lean fish courses. Ironically, the only caloric dish she enjoyed was macaroni, which was hardly fare for a world cruise.

Our birthday present for Jay was a pocket-sized New Testament. We'd already been discussing the Old Testament portrait of the Messiah in Isaiah Chapter 53.

"It takes chutzpah‡ to give this to you," I proffered between petit fours and coffee.

"Chutzpah is right!" Jay chuckled, stoking sherbet.

But he graciously received the very Jewish little book.

☆ ☆ ☆

Rio de Janeiro is synonymous with the sensual. Along Rio's undulating, white beaches, bronzed bodies are virtually worshipped as modern gods and goddesses. It's a city that's become a mecca for plastic surgery. Brazil's Dr. Ivor Pitanguy has been dubbed the 'Michelangelo of the face lift.' Jet-setters pay about £5,000 for a face lift. And leg reshaping or breast implants are now routine operations to make bodies more idolatrous for the beaches.

Perhaps the sheer physical beauty of Rio contributes to the sybaritic element, for nothing can compete with the city's overall spectacular panorama. If it were just another flat city, Rio perhaps could pass for any modern metropolis, but like Jerusalem, it is beautifully

(‡ *Yiddish and modern Hebrew for raw nerve, cheek*)

situated. Out of the glassy Guanabara Bay, as aquamarine in colour as the famous Brazilian gemstone, rise mountains resembling gigantic, emerald whales. Pristine white hotels and condominiums, surrounded by palms, pink blooms and mosaic sidewalks, sell for as much as half a million pounds a flat (but squalid shanties are also never too far away). The statue of Christ the Redeemer towers on a pinnacle half a mile above the bay. His arms are outstretched in perpetual blessing, and no matter where one ventures in Rio, bearings can be found by setting sights on the monumental Messiah.

We hurriedly downed two cups of syrupy Brazilian coffee in a sidewalk cafè before catching our bus up to Corcovado, the mount where the statue of Jesus stands on a natural pedestal 2,310 feet high. It was a harrowing climb and certainly not advisable for anyone suffering from vertigo. At one point, Corcovado became so steep that we had to continue the climb by mini bus. Then by foot. There were winding stairs to conquer before reaching the summit and its stupendous view.

The 100-foot monument with serene, stony face and pupiless eyes was erected by the Catholics in 1931.

A tourist who was wearing a star of David necklace approached me at the feet of Jesus. She was staring at the necklace that I was wearing that day. It was also a star of David but superimposed with a cross.

"Your necklace is so unusual," she ventured. "Why do you wear it?"

"Because I have found Him of whom Moses and the prophets wrote."

"Who?" Her expression was puzzlement.

"Him," I said, pointing up.

"Oh," she pondered, craning her neck to look straight up.

She walked away, but turned once more to contemplate the Jew, Jesus.

Chapter 4

South Africa

The gravitational pull of two continents seemed to lessen and then intensify again as the ship rolled through the South Atlantic during five days between Brazil and Africa. Our path through the sea had been peaceful, but approaching the tip of the massive African continent were the roughest waters of the entire cruise. Although the sky was brilliantly bathed, our entry was slowed by the choppy seas of the Cape of Good Hope, known ominously as the 'Cape of Storms'. to ancient mariners. The ship rocked, the cabins creaked, as the QE2 passed by lumbering barges and supertankers laden with middle-eastern oil. Small, struggling trawlers were pitched mercilessly in the blustery winds.

Many of the once wooden vessels of the Dutch East India Company were dashed to splinters on the Cape rocks where the Atlantic and Indian oceans meet. But on this day, gregarious gulls welcomed us, and tenacious tugs strained us closer to Cape Town as we watched, thoroughly wind-blown, from the Observation Deck above the bridge.

The advantage of arriving by ship is to imagine Africa and the Cape as they were first seen by European sailors. (A rest station was established at the bay as early as 1652 to relieve scurvy-ridden seamen.) And such an unforgettable sight it is! Sir Francis Drake once dubbed it the 'fairest cape in the whole circumference of the earth.'

Rising as a protective barrier behind Cape Town's gravity-defying skyscrapers was a 3,600 foot flat-top mountain, appropriately called 'Table Mountain'. Upon our arrival, it was ceremoniously spread with a tablecloth of fluffy cotton clouds.

As I gazed at this beauty, my spirit was apprehensive, realising that I was situated at the bottom of a giant continent of seething upheavals. I was about to encounter firsthand the agony of apartheid which so dominates the news. True to all accounts, South Africa appeared to be one of the world's most naturally endowed countries, with its mountains, minerals, flora and fauna, but like a beautiful woman with an internal cancer, the Republic of South Africa is also a shallow apology for its democratic claims. A minority of 4.3 million whites dominate the lives of 18 million blacks, 2.5 million 'Coloureds' (those of mixed race) and 850,000 Asians. All must carry racial identity cards. The whole population is registered to stop intermixture.

☆ ☆ ☆

We hired a car and drove south-east, visiting the barren, baboon-inhabited Cape Peninsula. It rather resembles a jutting lobster claw, with panoramic cliffs descending in a vector to the thrashing union of the Atlantic and Indian oceans. Along the way, stretches of broad, sandy beaches were reminiscent of the American South only a couple of decades ago. Sections were clearly segregated to racial quotas. Having grown up in Virginia, I can remember when blacks were automatically relegated to the backs of buses, but here in South Africa they had their own buses, albeit less attractive than those belonging to the whites. Separate buses. Separate toilets. Separate taxis. Everywhere facilities were separate, but not equal. Separate waiting rooms. Separate restaurants. Separate cinemas. Public notices both in English and Afrikaans often prohibited blacks and dogs.

But I also recall a sign on a stone church that seemed wonderfully incongruous in this segregated land. It proclaimed in bold letters, 'All races welcome'. This was so obviously the simple answer: when the Holy Spirit is allowed to infiltrate hearts, spiritual colour-blindness follows.

Upon asking a lot of questions, we learned that true believers in Jesus oppose apartheid. But, ironically, the roots of apartheid stem from a misapplication of the Bible in an effort to justify white domination. (How many times throughout history has the Word of God been twisted to justify some sect's position?)

The Dutch pioneers, the Boers, fought the black Bantus who came down from the north. Both whites and blacks claimed the newfound territory. Later, when the British came to the Cape, they abolished slavery. The Boers didn't agree. The Boers, whose descendants are today's Afrikaaners, trekked inland in covered wagons to escape British rule, British missionaries and their British talk of equality. The Boers fought the Bantus in bloody battles, and all they had to sustain them was a rigid religiosity. The Boers assumed they were God's new chosen people. They compared themselves to the ancient Israelites.

But the Israelites had been given a unique call to be a separate people in order to preserve God's ordinances and oracles. The Israelites had been forbidden by God to intermingle with other peoples, and so the Boers fancied that they shouldn't either. This attitude was the root of apartheid but a misapplication of Scripture as God had not called the Boers to be a separate people in the same way that he had ordained in the unique case of Israel.

The only way the Boers could survive and keep themselves pure was to stay absolutely separate from those whom they despised in their hearts as heathen savages. How totally different their attitude was from the universal love and hatred of slavery exhibited by the great missionary to Africa, David Livingstone. The spirit of that love was indivisible, as exhibited on the inscription of his tomb in Westminster Abbey: 'And other sheep I have, which are not of this fold: them also I must bring, and they shall hear my voice; and there shall be one fold, and one shepherd.' (*John 10:16*)

☆　☆　☆

In the eastern port of Durban, I experienced firsthand the arrogance of apartheid from a white shop owner. He was a stout man who sold African curios. When he observed that I was an American, he suggested that Washington should be more supportive of the South African government.

"After all," he said, "there's a common bond between my pioneer forefathers and your forefathers who settled America." He pointed out that both nations were founded by people who were looking for a new promised land.

I told him that I was trying to understand the complexities of South Africa's problems. I also told him that I was a Southerner who had grown up in a segregated society but that since the civil rights movement, the blacks in America had gained much of the equality the Constitution promises. The man suddenly screwed up his face and spat out his words: "In South Africa, the white man has just as much the same right to say 'this is my land' as white Americans say the United States is their land rather than the Indians!"

I should have known better than to get into a

conversation with a bigot, but I was also curious about what he believed. He leaned over the counter, leering into my face, and added: "You've got to understand something: whites here are not intruders. We've been here for hundreds of years. I'm an African just as much as the blackest African on this continent."

"I understand that," I said, rallying my thoughts. "And I think Idi Amin's genocide in Uganda was worse than your apartheid. But why can't the same freedoms and opportunities you have also be extended to your black neighbours?"

The shop owner drew up his chest arrogantly.

"I'll tell you why," he said. "I'll show you why."

He summoned a black worker from a back room. The old man — I suppose he was about 70 — walked out timidly. He wore a white apron.

"I have somebody here who thinks the government should give you the right to vote," the white man sneered in patronising tones.

I could hardly believe what was happening. My face burned with embarrassment for the way the old man was being humiliated.

"Why don't you tell the lady here the name of our prime minister."

The old man looked down at the floor and fooled nervously with his apron strings.

"Well, come on," the shop owner demanded impatiently. "Tell our visitor here the name of the prime minister. Don't you know it?"

The black man attempted a muffled answer. The shop owner sneered again and then turned quickly to me.

"You see, he's not smart enough to vote. None of them are. If he doesn't even know the name of the prime minister, how do you expect him to vote intelligently?"

"Could it be people like you have never given him the chance?" I said, looking apologetically after the black man, who retreated into the recesses of the back room.

"How do you expect him to be knowledgeable," I pressed, "when he is treated with no more dignity than a dog? I believe that Jesus is no respecter of persons. He values every person as a unique individual for whom he died, and he wants all people to be treated justly."

The white man now regarded me smugly. At the mention of Jesus, a prideful smile broke over his face.

"You won't find a more God-fearing nation than South Africa. We go to church every Sunday. We are staunch believers. We wouldn't even allow your corrupt television to be shown in this country until recent years. And we don't allow all the pornography that America allows. I tell you, we believe in God, and we do God's will! The white man represents civilisation and progress. If the blacks take over, our economy will be ruined."

I smarted under his blow about American TV and pornography, because I know it's true. Still, after having witnessed the humiliation of the black man, I wanted to fly to his defence. But it seemed a lost cause. The white man dismissed me with the wave of his hand as if the whole conversation had been a waste of his time. I left wondering if that man, and so many like him, could ever change.

Is it a realistic prayer? Alan Paton, author of *Cry, the Beloved Country*, has observed that the idea of race domination can become morally intolerable to the very people who support it. Slavery became repugnant to Western nations, and, with God's grace, white South Africa will learn, and is learning, to abhor apartheid, too.

During a tour to the historic white stronghold of Stellenbosch, one of the QE2's black passengers said she felt uneasy while dining at a tourist hotel. One of the ironies, or conveniences, of apartheid regulations is that black Americans are exempt. Japanese businessmen are considered white, too.

The day of our departure the *Rand Daily Mail* reported a bloody massacre in Zimbabwe in which several white missionaries had been gunned down by black guerillas using Russian weapons. The front-page story was a grim reminder of regional tensions, but the photograph said more than a thousand sermons on race relations. It pictured the anguished, tear-stained faces of the mission's black members over the brutal deaths of their white brothers. The newspaper photo seemed to be a commentary on St. Paul's words in Galatians 3:28 that in Christ there is 'neither Jew nor Gentile . . . male nor female' and it could be added today: there is neither black nor white.

Chapter 5

India

"The western god is worldly success. It has especially become an American cult. But it is too exclusive," asserted Hugh, our shipboard art and history lecturer.

Hugh continued to drone on in praise of Eastern religions, almost as if he were proselytising his worldly successful audience.

We were approaching the shores of India, which gave birth to Hinduism and Buddhism in addition to fostering Jains and Sikhs and playing host to Moslems, Zoroastrians and Christians. Only 2.5 per cent of the population is Christian, although Christianity is on the rise, particularly in the south.

Hugh devoted part of his Bombay preparatory lecture to the story of the Buddha, meaning 'enlightened one', how he was born a prince circa 565 B.C. in what is now Nepal, how he donned rags and abandoned his wife and family to discover truth. After many privations and wanderings, the Buddha meditated under a tree, where he found enlightenment. He began to preach the concept of 'nirvana', the total extinction of personality that can be reached only by those who are absolutely withdrawn from the world. The Buddha taught the transmigration of souls as part of the process of obtaining nirvana. He founded an order of monks, ate poisoned mushrooms and died. His last words were: 'Be ye lamps unto yourselves; work out your own salvation.'

Hugh's lecture was disturbing. He seemed to be overly enamoured with eastern philosophy. He also seemed blind to its inferior fruits of poverty and the caste system in which the masses do not see their lives as unique but as instalments in an insidious cycle of reincarnation.

"I've got a suggestion," Jay said wryly at lunch. "Why don't you work on Hugh?"

There was a playful twinkle in his eyes. His opinion of my evangelical antics seemed to be a mixture of good-natured tolerance, amusement and secret admiration.

"He seems to be pretty lost," Jay egged me on.

"Sometimes your discernment is uncanny," I noted.

"I bet Hugh sits cross-legged in his cabin every morning trying to obtain nirvana," Jay said, digging his fork into a splendid soufflé. He humoured me by adding, "I think he needs one of your tracts."

"You're right." I accepted the challenge. "But where will I find him?"

"Oh," Tiffany chimed in, "he usually hangs around in the casino."

☆　☆　☆

Hugh was alone in the casino jerking the handle of a one-armed bandit. He looked slightly annoyed at my intrusion.

"I heard your lecture this morning," I began, deciding not to mince words. "So what do you think of guru Jesus?"

"I've made a thorough study of the New Testament," Hugh replied. "Jesus was one of the greatest teachers who ever lived, but his teachings are impossible to keep."

"They're impossible to keep in your own power," I conceded, knowing full well that what Hugh said was true. "That's why he promised us the Holy Spirit —

to live in us and give us the power to keep his commandments." But even as I said that, I subconsciously wondered why my own life lacked the dynamic power of the Holy Spirit.

Hugh plopped another coin in his machine and anxiously pulled the handle. A few coins spewed out. He relaxed in satisfaction.

"You know," he mused, "all eastern religions acknowledge Jesus as a great teacher. Some even believe Jesus was an incarnation of one of their gods."

"But none acknowledges him to be God's only Son, nor do they consider him to be Lord," I said. "To them, he's just another god with no power to save."

Hugh rattled some coins restlessly in his palm.

"The thing I find untenable about Christianity — and I was brought up a good Anglican — is the concept of sin. Man is essentially good. Eastern thought is profound on this subject. Man's greatest 'sin,' for want of a better word, is that he's ignorant of his divine nature." Hugh's face took on an otherworldly mien. "We are all gods."

"Then how can you claim that Jesus was a great teacher?" I ventured. "You make him to be a liar."

"What?" Hugh was shocked.

"If you don't believe that man is inherently sinful, how can you call Jesus a great teacher? His disciple John said, 'If we say we have no sin, we deceive ourselves . . . and make God a liar.' Jesus also said, 'If you do not believe that I am Lord, you will die in your sins.'"

"The trouble with fanatics like you is that you say Jesus is the only way," Hugh muttered, feeding the slot machine another coin. "You shouldn't be so narrow. The world is a big place. There are many religions and ways to God, and who are you to say that Jesus is the only way?" He yanked the handle. Nothing came out.

"But I didn't say Jesus is the only way. Jesus said it. That's the difference. I'm not asking anybody to take my word for it. Jesus had the boldness to say, 'No one comes to the Father except by me.' So either he's telling the truth, or he's not the great teacher you claim him to be."

"We'll have to talk again," Hugh hedged.

I asked him if I could tell him a little story I'd heard that he could use for one of his future lectures. He agreed politely to listen . . .

Once there was a man who fell into a miry pit. There was no way to get out, and he cried day and night for help. Buddha came by, heard the man's anguished cries and yelled down this advice, "Work out your own salvation." Then Muhammad passed by, heard the man's cries and suggested that he should pray toward Mecca. But the man didn't have a compass. And then Jesus came by. He heard the man's cry of desperation and had compassion on him. Jesus ignored the dirt and slime and climbed down into the pit to rescue him. Then Jesus bore the man out on his own back. Which of the prophets do you think is worthy to be called Saviour?

☆　☆　☆

Mark Twain said it so well concerning the nation of India: "It is a curious people. With them, all life seems to be sacred, except human life."

The saying still holds true today. Our visual senses were assaulted with the hordes of humanity all 'locked' into their karmas — some rich and beautiful (a faraway gaze in their chocolate brown eyes and handsome faces), others wretchedly impoverished — sleeping, defecating and eating on the streets. In some quarters for their livelihood, men carry cots infested with bedbugs. They cry for money as volunteers lie on the cots to pay for the privilege of feeding the bloodsucking bugs.

The vultures are also well fed. In one of his lectures, Hugh had described the grotesque manner in which the Parsees dispose of their dead at the 'Tower of Silence'. The Parsees are descended from Persian Zoroastrians who came to India in the 7th and 8th centuries to escape Muslim persecution. They believe the four sacred elements of earth, air, fire and water must not be contaminated by the corpse of a mere human being. So the bodies of deceased loved ones are carried to the top of the tower and abandoned there on a metal grate. After the bones are picked clean by vultures, they fall through the grate into the tower, where they are consumed by chemicals.

A taxi deposited us at the entrance of the Parsee grounds, but as we walked up the potholed road, we were stopped by a stern man in a black fez. He refused our entry to the Tower of Silence. But we took some photos of two vultures circling in anticipation of their next meal.

The air pollution from the glut of cars, trucks and buses, dust and grit was so overwhelming, aggravated by the heat, that we were forced to carry our cloth dinner napkins to breathe through from time to time, literally to keep from choking.

On the way to visit Bombay's rather famous public laundry, government billboards and slogans painted in large red letters propagandised that 'Small Families Are in Your Best Interest'.

Bombay's largest public laundry could be viewed from atop a bridge where roving, ragged children accosted us with cupped hands, addressing us pleadingly in English as 'Mama' and 'Papa'. Our driver shooed them away contemptuously like flies and admonished us not to encourage any of the beggars with money or we'd be besieged.

The laundry's gray stone vats resembled a beehive clogged with mounds of drenched clothing while the Indian drones bent their backs and toiled endlessly. These washermen were born into their lowly caste and have no chance of working their way up the ladder of social success. Just as their fathers before them, they are bound in their profession by the caste organisation with no deviation from the traditional norms. As a member of this subcaste, a man is instilled with taboos. For example, he must squat on the floor and refuse food from any vessels in the home of, say, a middle class Indian. Such is the justice of the reincarnation theory.

Our rickety taxi, embellished inside with garish decals of elephant gods, took us up a back street past stalls of freshly strung flowers to be sacrificed to idols. It was festival time to some Hindu god. From a child, I had heard about idolatry in Sunday School but somehow it didn't connect with my occidental, Protestant mindset that idols are still worshipped today. Naively, I suppose I thought idolatry went out with the Ten Commandments and that a sacred cow was just somebody's cherished notion.

But near the temple a dark, squatting woman whose head was wrapped in a tattered shawl, was touting bunches of wilted grass to feed to a horned and humped sacred cow (with its supposed reincarnated soul).

She caught my eye and motioned for me to buy her dreary bouquet of grass. I politely declined, but she stood up, grabbed my arm and yelled something in Hindi. I decided to show her the cross around my neck as a reasonable defence for refusing her offer. She dropped my arm with a defiant yank.

Inside the temple, mendicants and fakirs chanted in

a loud commotion and rang foreboding bells to summon spirits. People prostrated themselves, stretching out their arms and pouring out their tortured souls with loud, piercing cries to a hideous elevated idol. Again, I felt a sickening shock, supposing naively, I guess, that such blatant idolatry was no longer tenable to modern minds but that it had become merely more subtle in the forms of pleasure, TV sets and the like. (In my cabin, I'd been reading through the Living Bible and was just becoming enamoured with God the Father and his holiness. I'd known Jesus from my infancy because of the blessing of godly parents. But the revelation of God the Father was becoming new to me.) So for a moment I felt only a fraction of the anger (or was it a profound sadness?) of what the Lord, a jealous God, must feel when he still sees His creation bowing, not to the Creator, but to the creation.

St. Paul explained the source of their worship very succinctly: "What pagans sacrifice, they offer to demons and not to God." Here also was a new insight into God's mercy — that He would deign to save any of us, who are all so prone to idolatry, whether it's a literal idol, or a person or an ideology.

The pseudo-holiness of the mendicants was reflected in their apparent blindness to the suffering and squalor around them. On the temple steps a young man with shaven head sat yoga-style in flowing white pants. Three sets of prayer beads hung artfully on his bare chest. His forehead was painted with red lines and yellow satanic-like horns. A slender woman with flowing black hair sauntered by proudly in a flaming red sari embroidered extravagantly in gold. Her piles of gold jewellery clanked in rhythm with her steps. She looked both regal and ethereal.

We asked the first mendicant if we could take his

photograph. He sat erect, smiled broadly and held out his prayer beads as if displaying wares. But an immediate 180-degree turn from the foot of the white marble temple steps revealed a picture of some of the most putrid living conditions imaginable. A ragged woman sat among hovels of mud, planks, jute and darting rats. Hinduism calls this disparity 'karma', or fate, and neither the man with the beads nor the rich beauty in red is compelled to elevate the condition of the wretch at their feet. It is her karma; conveniently, her plight really does not concern them.

Paradoxically, at a time when many Westerners have turned in vain to India's smorgasbord of religions, there is in India a serious turning to the Gospel of Jesus Christ. The masses of poor Indians, such as the ragged woman among the rats, need to hear the good news that their lives are unique before God and meaningful in this life time. That is why so many Indians flock to hear Christian messengers. They are attracted not only to the personality of Jesus, but Christianity gives them hope. There are eternal benefits if they accept the free gift of salvation through Jesus, but there are also very practical earthly social and economic benefits as well. Once they become children of God, by adoption through faith in Jesus, they become God's responsibility and can call upon him as a Father for all their needs.

In a word, Christianity for the Indian is deliverance.

By contrast, Hinduism, with its pantheon of gods, seems so backward that it's difficult to imagine sophisticated city dwellers bowing down to primitive idols. One might expect such behaviour from illiterate peasants in far-flung villages, but not from the educated Indian.

Such is not the case, however. At the famous Jain Temple, a worshipper appeared to be a dashing businessman dressed in a Continental-style designer suit. He toted a smart leather briefcase and bowed reverently before one of the many courtyard idols before ringing a bell to summon a god. He left a sacrifice of flowers at an altar.

A sign in English outside the garish temple entreated visitors with 'Inspiring Idols Inside'. We were told that Jainism is an ascetic religion founded in the 6th Century by a Hindu reformer. The more devout of the sect wear cumbersome wire mesh masks over their noses and mouths similar in principle to a surgeon's mask. But while the latter is used to ferret out germs, the Jain mask is a precaution against inhaling an insect, which might inadvertently kill a reincarnated soul. One young man who was a captive to such a mask proffered a string of red flowers to lay before an idol. I inwardly recoiled, grieved that he and others are held in bondage by such superstition. And yet I was happy to learn from an Indian Christian at Bombay's Anglican Cathedral that Christianity is freeing more captives in India today than in America, where many have become inoculated to the Gospel.

☆ ☆ ☆

Professor Vishnu was a teacher at an Anglican school in a gritty neighbourhood of Bombay. Only a few weeks prior to the cruise, I had met his daughter-in-law in America. We were delighted to receive a dinner invitation from the Vishnu family upon our embarkation near the grand arch commemorating the visit of King George V, one-time Emperor of India.

Mr. Vishnu's daughter, Roma, said she and her younger sister, Meena, would meet us at the dock at dusk. We liked Roma and Meena instantly. They were petite and delightfully chatty. They wore their long,

41

lustrous black hair in dogears like western schoolgirls.

"You speak English perfectly," I remarked, climbing into a taxi.

"Yes, since we grew up at the school, we have spoken English all our lives," Roma said. "We hardly ever use Hindi."

"Are you Christians?" I enquired, assuming they were since their father was employed by the Anglicans.

"Oh, no," Meena said matter-of-factly. "We're Hindu."

The drive took us into a deepening night that silhouetted shantytowns and a few dimly lit shops. The area was not illuminated by streetlights, and our driver, like most of his fellow motorists, didn't bother to use his headlights. Instead, he relied on his horn and brakes to navigate the dusty, narrow roads. Finally, after inching through a boisterous wedding party and passing a row of squalid sweet shops, the taxi stopped with a lurch.

"We're here," Meena chirped enthusiastically.

The school was enclosed by high stone walls. A security guard met the taxi, then waved us through rusty metal gates. The girls directed the driver to a dormitory, where the Vishnu family lived on the third floor. As we stepped onto the unpaved dusty compound, the ominous caws of India's ubiquitous black crows seemed to mock our arrival. Their silhouettes leered like vultures in the scrawny trees. A bat flew menacingly near our heads as we followed the girls up an open stairwell.

A stark corridor leading into their apartment displayed a solitary calendar with a lurid photo of a Hindu god. The main living room was three-sided with a heavy curtain that could be drawn across the front for privacy, but this night the curtain was fully open, revealing the black, moonless sky. The spartan furniture consisted of a black vinyl suite, utilitarian table and an oversized refrigerator in one corner.

Mr. Vishnu arose gingerly from his chair to greet us with a broad grin. His two front teeth were missing. Mrs. Vishnu sat silently on the sofa sorting bugs out of uncooked grains of rice.

"Mother is very weak from a recent illness," Roma said. "So tonight dinner is being prepared especially by Meena and myself."

The energetic sisters giggled and excused themselves to the kitchen but scurried back and forth to set the table for what appeared to be a feast. Meena summoned me to the kitchen.

"I want you to test the curry so we won't make it too hot for you and Peter," she giggled.

"Oh, go ahead and make it hot," Peter said adventurously.

I followed Meena through a bedroom of cots into a small makeshift kitchen. Roma was stirring a dish over a two-burner camp stove. I dodged the strings of laundry suspended overhead. Roma offered me a spoonful of her concoction.

"Oh," I winced, my eyes watering, "that's hot alright, but Peter will be very pleased. And we adore lamb curry."

"It's goat," Roma corrected me.

In addition to the saffron rice and goat curry, the girls had generously prepared a cold eggplant dish, freshly chopped vegetables and a pitcher of yellow soup that defied any previous culinary experience. All of this was accompanied by vegetables fried in batter, potato cakes and crisp pappadums. The oppressive sultry air and the spices worked together to create a terrific thirst, but Mr. Vishnu kept us well supplied with cold Cokes from his corner refrigerator and also with a thick, syrupy bottled drink made from mangoes.

All of this was finished off with syrup-drenched sweets purchased specially by messenger from the corner hovel outside the compound.

After dinner, the girls disappeared into the kitchen to wash up, but Mr. Vishnu seemed especially eager to talk about religion. He pulled up a chair directly in front of us, and grinned broadly.

"Well, now," he began, slapping his legs, "what would you like to ask me about Hinduism?"

He clearly wanted us to pump him. Peter mentioned that we were Christians.

"I always pray to Jesus," Mr. Vishnu grinned gratuitously, "and also to Krishna just to play it safe." He added a boast that he held a spiritual advantage over us Westerners. He claimed to have combined the best of Hinduism, Buddhism and Christianity into his own fail-safe credo.

I was stumped that an educated man such as Mr. Vishnu, who had taught at a Christian school for nearly 30 years, could so easily bow to rude idols and Jesus Christ at the same time.

Peter's manner was gently disarming.

"You say you worship Jesus, Krishna and other gods as well. But how do you rationalise the teaching of Jesus that no man can serve two masters?"

Mr. Vishnu chose to dismiss the question by beginning a discussion on temple sacrifices, which I then used as a springboard to mention mankind's very real need for atonement.

"The wonderful news is that God has already provided atonement for every person on this earth through the sacrificial blood of the Lamb — Jesus," I said, sincerely hoping that our amiable host would appropriate that atonement for himself.

But the professor revealed that he was trusting in his own good works and deeds for salvation. He again mentioned Lord Krishna and the Buddha.

"But," I interjected, "Jesus taught that any person who tries to enter into God's presence through a door other than Himself, that is, through some other prophet or religion, is a thief and a robber. In fact, one of his last warnings to his followers was that after him would come many false prophets who would lead many astray. Muhammad came. Many prophets and gurus came. Some of them even claimed to have received their revelations from angels, but no matter how good they sounded, Jesus nevertheless prophesied that they would all be clever counterfeits and wolves in sheep's clothing."

"Well," Mr. Vishnu laughed, "in my next life, we'll see if you were right."

"But," Peter said earnestly, "that may be too late. The Bible teaches that it's appointed unto man once to die, and then comes the Judgement. Reincarnation is a lie that prevents man from repenting of his sin here and now before he dies."

"I'm familiar with all the Scriptures you're mentioning," Mr. Vishnu said pensively, "but there are also many sacred Indian scriptures. Who is to say which one is right?"

"I'm sure the Indian scriptures contain many lofty thoughts and beautiful writings," Peter said, "but they are powerless to impart eternal life. But Jesus said: 'My words are spirit and life.' Also, Jesus said another important thing: not only did he predict that many false prophets would come after him; He also dared to say that all those who came before Him, such as Buddha, were also thieves and robbers. ‡

(‡ *"Verily, verily, I say unto you, I am the door of the sheep. All that ever came before me are thieves and robbers: but the sheep did not hear them. I am the door: by me if any man enter in, he shall be saved, and shall go in and out, and find pasture. The thief cometh not, but for to steal, and to kill, and to destroy: I am come that they might have life, and that they might have it more abundantly."* John 10:7–10

"All throughout the East," Peter continued, "you can venerate the bones of holy men. In fact, when we next go to Kandy, Sri Lanka, we're supposed to visit the Temple of the Tooth where Buddha's tooth is enshrined. Doesn't that tell you something? Buddha's bones can still be found, but the tomb of Jesus is empty! You can visit the tomb of Muhammad in Saudi Arabia, but the bones of Jesus have never been found, because He was the only holy man good enough to be resurrected! His resurrection was God's seal of approval that atonement for sins was accomplished on the cross."

Mr. Vishnu sat silently for a moment. What he said next was bittersweet, because it indicated that he was on the threshold of belief in Jesus Christ. But, sadly, his words were also awesome, because either consciously or unconsciously, the Indian professor echoed the exact words that King Agrippa said to the Apostle Paul.

"You almost persuade me," he mused, thus echoing the ancient words of Agrippa which have been repeated through countless lands and generations by individuals unwilling to yield to the lordship of Jesus Christ.

☆　☆　☆

Back on the ship, there was a run on the laundry room to wash the Indian grit from our clothes. As I was leaving with my bundle of clean clothes, I ran into Sean O'Reily, the library steward. He grabbed me by both shoulders and shouted unabashedly, "Praise the Lord!"

"While I was in Bombay," he enthused, "I met the most fantastic group of believers, and I plan to go back and join them just as soon as I can terminate my duties on this ship!"

Something in my spirit went off like an inner alarm bell.

"Tell me about the group," I urged.

"They're all fairly young. Some are Americans. Some are Europeans. They live together in a house and share everything. They're poor and collect alms on the streets. One of the brothers was sick, and everyone was caring for him. They were so loving. They really took me in, too. In fact," he laughed, "they hardly let me go. They kept telling me how much they needed me."

Since I already knew Sean was starved for regular fellowship, I was doubly anxious that he not join just any group to fill a void. He kept repeating how the group had shown him love — the missing element in his lonely life. He began to tell me about their methods of asking for alms among the other beggars on the Bombay streets. He said he planned to sell his bungalow in Britain to help them financially.

"Do you have any of their literature?" I asked.

"They gave me plenty of pamphlets," Sean said. "I'll let you read them the next time you're in the library."

He strode off happily toward the Quarter Deck Library, where one of his duties was selling foreign stamps for letters and postcards.

As I watched Sean O'Reily walk down the passageway, I hated to try to burst his bubble. But something was warning me that he should not join that group under any circumstances. At the time, I didn't know exactly what that 'something' was that was warning me. That inner red light, I was to learn, is the anointing, or unction of the Holy Spirit, that abides in all believers and teaches us all things (*1 John 2:27*).

The anointing within — the still, small voice of God — was also warning Sean, but at the time, he was too emotionally attached to this new group to listen.

Chapter 6

Singapore — Malaysia

We sailed a few evenings later from Colombo, Sri Lanka, during a spectacular lightning storm, but by the next morning the Bay of Bengal had settled into a sultry, humid sea. It was far too hot to venture out on the sun decks, and we soon adopted a lethargic mood like the slow, rippling waves outside our porthole. As we lay on our berths reading and writing letters, Peter suddenly grew weary of the piped-in music and took out his short-wave radio, propping it against the porthole.

"I might just be able to tune in Radio Australia," he muttered as he fiddled with the knobs. There was a long burst of static, and suddenly a woman's voice could be heard . . . "U.K. relay ready for caller?" It seemed to come from nearby.

"What's that?" I asked.

"Apparently, I've somehow tuned in to the ship's radio."

Just then the ship-to-shore operator announced that a circuit to London had been established and instructed a Mrs. Thomas that her party was on the line.

Haltingly, the voice of Mrs. Thomas came on. She began to speak in controlled sobs to a relative in England, telling the shocking news that her husband had just died on board. She herself was virtually in a state of shock. She said her husband had been perfectly well at the start of the cruise. But a few days previously, he had suffered a heat stroke, and now he was dead. She was seeking advice on what to do with his body —

whether to have it shipped home or buried at sea. She said a doctor had advised her to stay on the QE2, that to interrupt the journey suddenly might only aggravate her state of shock. After a few more tearful words, Mrs. Thomas terminated the call.

The entire radio transmission had lasted only a few minutes, but the surprise of it left us staring at each other in amazement. Peter admitted some embarrassment at having overheard such an intimate conversation. But we felt that the timing was no happenstance.

I began a quick check of the passenger list and confirmed that this woman was aboard. But how could we comfort her?

☆　☆　☆

Singapore lay on the misty horizon like a mirage of Manhattan. Slender skyscrapers sprouted up from this tiny island at the very tip of the Malay Peninsula, signifying her fantastic wealth. Economically, Singapore has the highest standard of living in all Asia, except Japan, with a per capita income nine times that of India and six times that of China.

The air-conditioned shopping centres lured passengers with the extra duty-free inducement. Everything electrical confronted those who love high tech toys. One could buy jeans, jade or jewellery. Or a duty-free Swiss watch. Entire shops were devoted to lizard and alligator handbags, wallets and briefcases, not to mention British woollens, Malay silver and beaded evening wear.

Nowhere did we see more culturally diverse peoples thriving together on each others' abilities. Singapore's heterogeneous population is divided among Chinese (who are the majority), Malays, Indians, Pakistanis and other ethnic groups. Mandarin, Malay and Indian dialects are spoken, but English is the cohesive language of trade and administration. This city-state of about two million inhabitants is an example of an industrial success. Nowhere, in our limited stay, did we see traces of poverty. Though resembling the modernity and wealth of Manhattan, Singapore was much cleaner. Hugh warned us not to litter or else incur hefty fines of several hundred dollars. Also, the Singapore government is well known now for the world's strictest laws against drug traffic. Even long hair on men is frowned upon.

Judging from its architecture and sophistication, except for an occasional pedishaw, we hardly realised we were visiting an oriental city. The skyline includes the inevitable hotels such as the Hilton, Hyatt and Sheraton. But the city still boasts the old world charm of the Raffles Hotel as a landmark distinctly Singaporean where one can imagine Somerset Maughan still sipping one of his slings. The immaculately white St. Andrew's Anglican Cathedral in the heart of the city was one of the few clues that the British ruled for about 140 years. Also singular to Singapore are the Tiger Balm Gardens — a gauche oriental mixture of plants and Disney-like comic animals, gaudy gorillas and obese buddhas moulded in plastics.

☆ ☆ ☆

Singapore may have bedazzled us with its opulence and modernity, but Peter also admitted to disappointment at the absence of turbanned sultans, real non-plastic tigers and British officers in solar topees. Those images had been his boyhood impressions of Malaysia from books and stamp collecting.

"Somewhere behind all these glass banks and hotels,

there must be something that looks like the Far East," he grumbled. Determined to find the 'real' Malaysia, he made reservations for a tour that would take us across the Straits of Johore.

Our bus left the quayside and was soon crossing the long causeway linking Singapore with its neighbour state of Johore. The contrast was dramatic, and Peter seemed pleased with the new photogenic scenery. Instead of a crowded island of office buildings, we now sped along tarmacadam roads through lush, almost jungle, territory. The homes and villages were largely makeshift, with bamboo curtains, thatched roofs and primitive patches of vegetable gardens carved from the dense undergrowth.

At a countryside hotel, we were led into a verandahed dining room already occupied by an impatient group of German and Dutch tourists. With expectations of exotic Malaysian cuisine such as satays roasting on their skewers, we sat down at one of the long dining tables. A parade of barefooted waiters distributed the first course. Peter's face was a picture of consternation as they laid before us bowls of alphabet soup.

"We come all the way to the jungles of Malaysia, and what do they serve us? Campbell's soup!" he quipped.

I had to laugh and several of the others seated at our table were also laughing, but the woman to my right ignored the camaraderie. Her eyes were concealed by dark glasses and her unkempt hair was partially wrapped beneath a scarf.

"Are you enjoying the cruise?" I asked. She continued to gaze down at her soup bowl and seemed reticent to reply.

"To tell you the truth," she sighed, "I'm still in a state of shock. You see, my husband died several nights ago on the ship."

My soup spoon halted midway in its trajectory. I was

sitting next to Mrs. Thomas!

"You'll have to excuse me," she continued in a soft, confiding voice, "but I'm not very much of a conversationalist at the moment. It's been such a dreadful shock . . . and being so far from home . . ."

Her voice trailed off, and she resumed sipping absently at the soup. My mind raced for words to respond. My immediate thought was to blurt out, "I know! I know all about it!" but that didn't seem appropriate. God had surely arranged our seating together, so to him I laid claim to strength for the right words.

She unburdened the whole, sad story, how she and her husband had been ballroom dance partners and this was to have been the trip of a lifetime for them. Her husband had promised when the QE2 docked in Hong Kong to buy her the most exquisite ballgown they could find. And then, suddenly, came the unexpected stroke, apparently aggravated by the heat and strenuous touring of several days in India and Sri Lanka. His last request had been for her to stay on the ship as far as Hong Kong to buy the dress.

Her husband was to be buried at sea the following morning. I encouraged her to lean upon the Lord, who is always available when we call on Him, but this simple suggestion seemed to trouble her. She was under condemnation for having left the church years ago, and she was making the mistake that so many people do in believing that it would be unmannerly now to ask God for help.

"I still believe in Jesus," she mused, "but I feel like I've lost contact with Him through the years. It wouldn't be fair to ask for His help now . . . now when I need Him."

"Oh, God's not like that!" I said softly. "If you had neglected some friend for years, you might be embarrassed to call on her for help. But God's ways and thoughts are higher and more noble than ours. He waits patiently on us without grudging. Thank God, Jesus isn't a fair weather friend!

"The Bible teaches that it's never too late to renew contact with the Lord. He's promised never to leave us, nor forsake us, even when we forsake Him. And He's the only one who can fill the void in your life right now, if you invite Him in."

"I know you're right," Mrs. Thomas said, dimly smiling for the first time. "I guess I just needed somebody to tell me."

Chapter 7

China

Like the dignified entrance of royalty, the QE2 entered Hong Kong, the 'Beautiful Harbour', with an entourage of junks, freighters, water taxis, snub-nosed ferries and tugs, cargo ships, hydrofoils and flotillas of sampans. The surrounding high-rise hotels and commercial buildings on Hong Kong Island and Kowloon peninsula formed walls of wealth scaling seemingly every square foot, and all of this was destined to be handed over on a silver platter to Communist China in just a sliver of time — 1997.

Before our arrival, we were briefed at a group meeting on the do's and don'ts of travelling in the People's Republic of China, where we would be spending three days on a shore excursion in Canton. Ours was to be the largest group ever to visit China — over 600 passengers had signed up.

"Leave your suitcases outside your cabin door, and they'll be picked up in the morning and delivered to your hotel in Canton," our QE2 liaison said. Peter gave me a relieved nudge at those instructions.

"No border hassles," he said. "Our suitcases are to be delivered separately!"

We were relieved because we planned to take a secret cargo: 10 copies of the New Testament in Chinese and scores of John's Gospel covered in red to resemble Chairman Mao's Little Red Book.

The Bibles which we acquired in Hong Kong are officially banned in China, so they had to be safely packed away. We stashed them inside a hosiery bag, a toiletry case and pockets of one of Peter's jackets all in one suitcase. Then we locked the case, prayed over it, and set it outside the cabin door with our other bag to be picked up by the stewards. According to our instructions, we thought that would be the last we'd see of the cases until our Canton hotel room.

The telephone rang at 4 a.m.

"The dining room is ready to serve breakfast," our tour liaison announced.

It was at that early morning breakfast that we first met Jonathan Saunders, a waiter who had been on leave from the ship and had just flown out to Hong Kong to rejoin her. He had been reassigned to our area of the restaurant, working from the same station as Oliver and Charlie. The latter were late, so Jonathan, a talkative fellow, served us coffee. I was impressed immediately by his outgoing nature.

"Well, well, well! Good morning," he enthused, although it was still black as night. "It's good to see some young people on board." He looked to be about 30 himself. He had dark, Mediterranean features, curly black hair, but a definite English accent. He hummed a blithe tune as he poured steaming coffee into our cups.

He admired the gargantuan cross necklace that I was wearing against a stark, black dress, making me appear somewhat like a cleric or a modern nun.

"Oh, you can't miss it, can you?" I said, fingering the necklace. "I'm wearing this oversized cross to make a statement. I plan to flaunt it in China, because true, Bible-believing Christians there have been suppressed."

Jonathan seemed to be fascinated with my premeditated effrontery.

"But it's not just the officials whom I want to confront with this cross," I said. "The open display of this necklace might encourage underground Christians if they see it."

"I'm from Malta, and we've got some beautiful, very distinctive crosses there," Jonathan said, leaning against the waiters' station. "But I don't remember too much about Malta. My Mother was born there, but my father's English, and I've lived most of my life either in England or at sea." He paused. "I was confirmed in the Anglican church, but I don't ever go to church. It just doesn't have any meaning to me."

Oliver and Charlie arrived with yawning protests to serve our light breakfast, followed by Jay and Tiffany, who were full of excitement and anticipation. But Jonathan kept hovering near us and breaking into quick bits of conversation whenever he could leave his own tables. Although he was just a nominal Christian, he revealed a real concern about the occult. He sensed there was something forbidden about it.

"One time a psychic medium sat at one of my tables and gave me a whole lot of books and tapes to listen to. The medium kept telling me that I could have great psychic powers, but," Jonathan added with a frown, "I didn't buy it. I'd already heard enough from the wife."

"Your wife's in the occult?" Peter asked.

"Yeah, she's the seventh daughter in seven generations. You know, that means she's supposed to be born psychic. Her mother was a gypsy who predicted her own death. She predicted that on a certain day she would be killed in an automobile accident, and she was."

"Oh, that makes me mad," I said, getting dramatic. "A demonic spirit makes those predictions in the first place. And then if the people are gullible enough, they give in to the demon's destructive plan for their lives. They actually allow the plan to come to pass by passively giving in to the lying suggestions!"

"Christine," Jay interrupted, somewhat bemused. "I'm sure you have a tract on the subject to give him."

"I certainly do! Did you know, Jonathan," I added, "that the Bible specifically forbids any traffic with the occult? As a protection to keep us from deception, the Bible condemns astrology, trying to communicate with the dead, fortune telling, enchantments, witchcraft, water dousing, automatic writing, all those kinds of things. To even dabble with any of them is dangerous."

"I'd like to talk with you some more," Jonathan said.

After breakfast, he startled us by his open-mindedness to seek truth.

"Look, while you're in China, do you have anything I can study, like a Bible, or something?"

"We certainly do!" From my pocket, I pulled out a potpourri of tracts and found one exposing the dangers of the occult. We also gave him a paperback copy of the Gospel of John in modern English entitled, *Who Was Jesus?*

"Thanks," he said enthusiastically, thumbing through the new information. "I'll read all of these things, and we'll talk some more when you get back."

☆　☆　☆

Our trek into China began at the Hong Kong train station, where young and fashionable representatives dressed in neat navy blazers escorted us through the New Territories. At the border state of Lowu, we were transferred to a Chinese train.

The difference became quickly apparent as we met our new guides on the communist side of the border. They were dressed alike — both the men and the women — in baggy Mao suits and unisex black slippers.

"Welcome, friends" was the common greeting of the guides who were to accompany us so closely that we inadvertently found ourselves referring to them as guards.

"Follow us, please," they beckoned toward a battery of inspection stations. Officials in green uniforms were scrutinising passports and visas.

I took one last, rather wistful, look at the British flag flying on the other side of the Lowu bridge. Then I gazed up at the ominous Chinese flag — the colour of the blood of countless martyrs who have died for their faith under communism.

We were ushered into a plain waiting room devoid of any decorations, only white slipcovered sofas and chairs, where tea was served from large, utilitarian kettles. Mr. Chang, our own guide, unexpectedly informed us that all groups would line up by numbers for suitcase inspections before boarding the train.

Peter and I gulped nervously from our teacups. So, the suitcases were not to go directly to our hotel after all! Uttering prayers under our breath that the Bibles would not be confiscated, we inched up in a line that seemed an eternity.

Finally, when it was our turn, the grim inspector ignored our hand luggage and the other case and asked only to see inside the bag that happened to contain all the Bibles.

Peter seemed amazingly cool. He smiled, pulled out his key and unlocked the case. Strangely, the inspector lifted the lid only a few inches and peeked timidly inside. His behaviour was mysterious, as if he were afraid that something like a jack-in-the-box would jump out and startle him. He quickly closed the case and drew himself up.

"Inspection over!" he announced perfunctorily.

The Bibles were safely through.

☆　☆　☆

As we sipped perfumed tea and ate boxed lunches of strange meats, fried rolls, green apples and cold pastries, the train sped through land cultivated to the horizon. Bending over their crops were the workers — peasants as they proudly call themselves — wearing pointed straw hats. There were no machines in sight, just plenty of hands, primitive tools, buckets on yokes and water buffaloes.

Mr. Chang, assisted by an everpresent Miss Chew, presented each of us a propaganda newspaper printed in English. The headlines were predictable, such as 'China Determined to Liberate Taiwan' or, 'Russian Imperialism Foe of China'.

At the Kwangchow (Canton) railway station, hundreds of onlookers were lined up to peer at us over the shoulders of police guards. We were curiosities. Most young people brought up under this regime had not seen foreigners until trade was opened up more recently.

Inside the station the first of many gigantic colour portraits of the late Chairman Mao Tse-tung confronted us. His ubiquitous countenance has come to symbolise the transfer from a long-held belief in ancestor worship to the adoration of the state with the chairman as its godhead. Mao's monotonous face was everywhere, or paired with portraits of his predecessors. Often the portraits in hotels or communes depicted Mao gazing toward the heavenlies like a religious prophet while Chinese youths sat adoringly at his feet. Once perhaps the most aesthetic people on the face of the earth, with a history of incomparable art, the Chinese communists have sacrificed ornamentation for visual political clichés.

☆　☆　☆

Our enormous hostelry of 1,233 rooms, the Tung Feng, was spartan but certainly adequate. It was rather Stalinesque in architecture, like a mirage out of Moscow. Our room contained two double beds overhung with mosquito nets, dusty armchairs, a desk, a plate of mandarin oranges, a package of unfiltered cigarettes, a vacuum bottle of hot water, tea and lidded teacups and plastic bedroom slippers. China may be a classless society, but the English label on our soft pink toilet tissue read, 'High Class Toilet Paper'.

Outside the window, I gazed down upon a community of poorly lit homes with unpaved sidewalks. Barefooted children were ragged — not quite the picture of utopic China painted by so many journalists.

There was to be a banquet in the hotel dining room during which Chinese officials would make effusive speeches and toast friendship to the some 20 countries represented by QE2 passengers. We were told to convene in the lobby at 5:30p.m. for a 'friendship party', but that the actual banquet would begin at 6.00. We were exhausted from the early morning travel and border strain. We overslept from a nap and awoke at 5:30. A nap seemed a perfectly normal liberty for tourists to take.

However, at 5:45, there was a ring on the old-fashioned telephone in our room.

"This is Mr. Chang. You are not down here." His voice sounded strained, as if to say, come immediately.

"Oh, do forgive us," I said. "We took a little nap."

"You must come at once!" he asserted. Then there was an abrupt click.

The Chinese, we were learning, live rigidly by the clock, since the entire nation has been galvanised into political consciousness. The factories, communes and clinics have been highly systematised. It is a thoroughly controlled society, with less personal freedoms than

Russian communism. (Even the number of children that a couple can have is strictly controlled.) Many of the three million Cantonese arose sharply at 6a.m. to music piped from loudspeakers. We were told that these morning reveilles were entitled, for example, 'I Drill Oil for My Motherland' or, 'A Song in My Heart for the Party'. Other martial music blared from loudspeakers built into street lamps. The one possession that just about every worker owned was a watch.

The banquet progressed through many courses of splendid Cantonese cuisine as we sat at round tables interspersed with our escorts. The fowl and the fish were served with their heads intact. No chopsticks were presumed upon us, although I rather missed being offered them. Instead, we were each provided one very plain fork.

To my right, young Miss Chew glowingly espoused the superiority of communism over the old China. She fielded questions with much zeal.

One of the opulent women in our group asked Miss Chew if she ever desired to wear make-up or jewellery.

She smiled tolerantly, saying, "We believe that make-up and jewellery are for little girls to play with."

However, since China has been more and more opened up to the West, bourgeoisie cosmetics and hair styles are gradually being allowed again in some places.

"And what of your religious beliefs?" I ventured, knowing full well that the Communists have a few 'show-case churches' to feign freedom of religion. "Where are your evangelical Christian preachers and Buddhist monks now?"

Her answer was terse, and I detected a slight irritation in her gaze as she answered: "Many of them have other jobs now."

Then she looked away. The subject was closed.

☆　☆　☆

We felt somewhat frustrated that so far we had been unable to disperse Bibles as we toured only the places that our hosts wanted us to see. Our vigilant escorts stayed on our heels and whenever any of us strayed slightly off course, Mr. Chang or Miss Chew nervously pursued us pleading: "This way, friends! You must stay with the group!" Even when I went to the toilet while touring, Miss Chew followed me and waited outside the stall.

"I've got an idea," Peter said after the banquet. "Let's go for a walk outside. It's very dark tonight. We may be able to distribute some Bibles if we're careful."

By then our guides had gone home, and most of our fellow wined-and-dined tourists had retired to their rooms. So we ventured unhindered out of the hotel, passing a guard station where incoming cars were monitored, and feeling somewhat like escaping inmates.

Few cars passed us on the wide, unlit boulevard. Workers on bicycles peddled their way to and from night shifts. Pedestrians regarded us warily, perhaps as 'foreign devils' (a term first applied to missionaries).

"I would love to distribute these Gospels right here on the street," Peter said, "but I don't know if the people will receive them or trust us."

"Let's try anyway," I said, reaching for a publication from my pocket.

A fortyish couple was approaching us.

"Excuse me," Peter motioned. He folded his hands as if in prayer. I held out my large cross necklace as a silent explanation, and Peter offered the man a red-jacketed Gospel of John. The faces of the Chinese couple were blank. The man took the booklet and thumbed quickly through the pages, holding them up to the moonlight. He muttered something to the woman, then thrust the Gospel back into Peter's hand. His face was still expressionless. He held up his hand as if to say no thank you. Either he didn't care or he knew from years of propaganda that he wasn't supposed to read that little book. They walked briskly away.

"Well, that didn't work," Peter said ruefully. "How can we reach these people?" He thought for a moment. "Wait a minute," he said excitedly: "I've got an inspired idea! A lot of the older people might remember the missionaries, right?"

"Right!"

"And if they were ever exposed to Christianity, they'd probably remember some of the tunes of Christian hymns. So let's sing!"

"Right here on the street?" I asked.

Somehow, though, we weren't afraid, although I suppose it was a ridiculous sight: two Westerners standing on a dark Canton street corner, surrounded by billboards of Chairman Mao, singing and whistling oldies but goodies such as 'Onward Christian Soldiers'. We kept singing until we ran out of hymns that we could recall.

Suddenly, a group of men — about 10 — was approaching us. The man who appeared to be the leader — I'll call him Dr. Wang to protect his identity — had an amicable smile. He began to address us through a younger man in the group who was more articulate in English. He said they were employed at a local hospital. Dr. Wang pointed to my cross pendant.

"Are you Christian?"

The others in the group stopped chatting among themselves and began to listen to the conversation that was developing through the interpreter. We could hardly believe the opportunity that was being given to us to talk about Jesus to a group of professionals who said, as far as we could gather, that they had just finished attending an operating theatre seminar on acupuncture.

"Yes, we're Christians," I said, surprised by my

boldness, and clasping my cross. I directed my answer through the translator.

"I was once Christian," Dr. Wang said in broken English, adding, "Missionaries. Missionaries."

So apparently he had studied at some Christian mission before the Communists expelled all foreign missionaries. We were disheartened to hear him say that once he was a Christian, but the thought also occurred to us that perhaps he still was a Christian, but in secret. I had read about Christians in communist lands who remain secret believers so they can aid other Christians, many of whom are languishing in prisons. Then there are many who still secretly believe but who are not willing to pay the price of letting it be known publicly.

"Do you remember anything about Jesus?" I asked Dr. Wang, going through the interpreter again. He shook his head affirmatively.

To the translator (who looked to be a nurse or resident doctor), I asked: "Have you ever heard of Jesus?"

"Of course, I've heard about Jesus, but Christianity is for capitalists."

"Oh, no, Christianity is not just for capitalists," Peter insisted, "Christianity is for all people, whether they live under capitalism or communism."

To Peter's well-timed comment, I added: "Jesus was the perfect member of the working class. Although He was the Son of God, He humbled Himself and worked with his hands as a carpenter. He never owned any possessions. He never owned a house. Jesus taught that if somebody steals your jacket, you should also give him your coat. He once commanded a rich man to sell everything he owned to give to the poor . . . would you mind telling all of that to Dr. Wang?"

The young translator obliged as Dr. Wang continued grinning with each sentence. Was it a polite smile of an outgoing personality, a contemptuous grin of a backslider, or a secret believer's front? It was difficult to discern.

"Bible is just story," Dr. Wang spoke again in English, egging us on.

Now all the Chinese in the group gathered closer around us and seemed absolutely absorbed. None of them interjected any arguments and the street seemed perfectly still, as if we were in a time warp, with no distractions. To refute Dr. Wang's statement that the Bible is just a story-book, I decided to take a certain tack, again asking the young man to translate.

"Do you know where Jerusalem is?" Everyone nodded yes.

"The Bible teaches that Jesus is coming back from heaven. And He's coming to Jerusalem. The Bible says He will set up a world government there. Not in Bejing. Not in London. Not in New York, but in Jerusalem.

"You Communists want a world government, and that's exactly what the Lord Jesus has in mind. But it will not be communism. There will be peace, and there will be no more war and no more arms. There will also be a big difference between the world government of Jesus and that of communism. Do you know what that difference is?"

"Tell us," Dr. Wang said, appearing to be enjoying himself immensely.

"The difference between communism and Jesus' world government will be that everybody on earth will worship God." I pantomimed my point by folding my hands as if in prayer and bowing my head reverently.

"And the knowledge of God will fill the earth as the waters cover the sea," Peter added. "Jesus is God, and one day soon, when He returns, all nations will bow at His name, including the People's Republic of China!"

The translator's voice may have been tinged with unbelief or sarcasm, and yet we sensed that the main thought penetrated. Dr. Wang laughed to break the silence and shook our hands as if to say the dialogue was over. Peter asked if he could take a picture of us with his flash, and Dr. Wang was agreeable. In fact, he suddenly took out a scratch piece of paper and wrote down his name and address and thrust it into my hand.

"Send me picture," he demanded.

I promised we would and wanted to give him a Bible, but I also sensed that it would embarrass him, or possibly even endanger him in front of his comrades. Since I had his address, I immediately thought of an alternative plan to send him a Bible with the photograph.

His parting words were warm, "You friends with the Chinese people." He clasped our hands again. "You friends."

Ecstatic with this encounter, we continued ambling along the boulevard, distributing Bibles where we could, and when we returned to the hotel around 11p.m., our burden of Bibles was considerably lightened.

✩　✩　✩

About 11:30p.m. Tiffany rapped on our door.

"Where have you guys been? Come on over and let's brew some tea. Jay is really bored."

He was pacing the floor, in fact. Already, one day in the controlled Chinese society was irritating his independent nature.

"We've got to break away from our group," Jay grumbled. "Does the tourist to China see anything he can rely on, or are we merely going to see what they want us to see? I'm tired of dodging Miss Chew and Mr. Chang every minute. In the morning, let's demand a taxi for the four of us. I want to see the real China."

"Sounds like a great idea," we agreed, knowing this would give us more opportunities to distribute Bibles. But in the morning (it was a Sunday), our guides evasively insisted that we couldn't hire a taxi.

"Why not?" Jay demanded defiantly. He was at his arrogant best. "The sign in the lobby clearly says, 'Taxis for hire'. The four of us want to spend a day exploring Canton on our own."

"We will check with the authorities," Mr. Chang said, but in a few minutes he returned with the announcement that a taxi hire would be quite impossible.

But while our group shopped in the government tourist store filled with exquisite bourgeois merchandise, we managed to slip away and walk unescorted along some of the back streets. The object was to visit real Chinese shops to check the availability of consumer goods. The standard items were Mao suits, slippers, watches, alarm clocks and sweaters, while our compatriots from the tour were offered hand-embroidered silk jackets, enamel work, gold and silver encrusted jewellery and porcelain.

We felt depressed by the monotony and dehumanising sameness, in addition to the absence of pets, street touts, cafès. We peered into the doorways of some homes. Many were wet and littered and full of flies.

Before returning to the group, we passed a building that was once a church. The cross on the steeple was broken and dangling horizontally. I wondered if the people remembered the original purpose of the building, which was probably now a civic centre, school or some other institutional building.

We lunched at a restaurant that was cordoned into at least three sections. The poor masses were crowded into what looked like a Chinese version of a lower class pub-lunch. They sipped tea from cracked cups and raked in their rice with chopsticks from unadorned bowls held just under their chins. Our section of the restaurant was clearly segregated and middle class in decor and fare. But on a higher floor (which we hurriedly explored) there was even a grander upper class banqueting room with antique furnishings and red velvet cushions, obviously reserved for government officials and their parties.

☆   ☆   ☆

An air of religiosity abounded at the rigorously progressive kindergarten at a showcase commune. It was almost like attending Sunday School. But the message was exultation of 'the good guys' (the party leaders) and defamation of 'the bad guys' (anti-party cliques or those generally out of favour). On the kindergarten walls, glowering portraits of Mao, Lenin, Marx and Engels kept vigil over the 175 youngsters, ranging in age from 3 to 6.

For our observation, the children ran a relay race, but they didn't carry a common stick. It was a Red torch. When they played tug-of-war, the instructor allowed no side to win. That would encourage rivalry, and there is no room for rivalry in the People's Republic of China, we were told. Even the puppet show was yet another lesson from Mao thought. And one of their many patriotic dances was choreographed explicitly to depict the throwing of hand grenades in defence of the motherland. The little spirits of the children were being moulded, but also starved of variety, nursery stories and fantasies. All culture seemed to be reduced to propaganda. With numbed horror, I watched the plump faces of three-year-olds, like little programmed robots, espousing their love for the party.

The pianist who accompanied the children while they sang political songs played an old upright piano made by an American manufacturer. Peter speculated that perhaps the piano had been confiscated from a mission when all churches were closed during the Great Proletarian Cultural Revolution of 1966–69, and when posters proclaimed, 'Hang God!' It was during this dark period that Mao encouraged youths born after the establishment of the republic to experience revolution for themselves. So the young 'Red Guards' terrorised Christians and wiped out all traces of 'imperialist missionaries' by burning Bibles, smashing pews, disgracing pastors (jailing or exterminating them with trumped-up charges) and therefore forcing believers to meet clandestinely and never in the same place.

The Cultural Revolution was the end of outward forms of worship. Many joined the government's counterfeit religious Three-Self Movement, but the rest of the church went underground.

My thoughts turned poignantly to Ni Shu-tsu, better known as Watchman Nee, one of the greatest Christians of this century. Born east of Canton in Swatow in 1903, Nee was a third-generation Christian who became the most brilliant leader of the indigenous church continuing even after Mao Tse-tung declared the establishment of the People's Republic of China on October 1, 1949. Nee knew that time was short, and he kept trying to equip the saints for persecution ahead. His seminars and sermons were published and appreciated by millions in the West, though Watchman Nee was probably never aware of the profound world-wide effect of his writings. He died in a communist labour camp after 20 years of imprisonment for his faith during which he never betrayed his Lord. Ironically, it was because of this Chinaman's book, *The Normal Christian Life*, that I, a Westerner, was firmly a believer in Jesus. I, an occidental, was forever indebted to an oriental for his lucid exposition of the Gospel, which was further proof of Christianity's ability to transcend all cultures.

Now the unevangelised children of Nee's people took a break from entertaining QE2 passengers to engage in odd jobs. Child labour was still quite evident in China. Some of the tots hoed a garden; others threaded teabags for the state at tiny worktables.

"This teaches them an appreciation for working for the state," our kindergarten guide explained.

"They were once taught things like flowers, birds, insects, fishes and animals or tales about ants moving soybeans and eagles catching chickens," the guide said, reading from an official paper.

"But since the cultural revolution, guided by Chairman Mao's teachings, we have made transformations in education. Much attention has been paid to educating the children with Mao Tse-tung thought from their early childhood."

☆　☆　☆

The message-making was by no means subtle at a people's commune that same Sunday. It could have been any day of the week. In China, there is no one day of rest. We were told that the peasants are given free time, but it could be any day of the week. We passed no former churches, no pagodas, no temples. We were plied with statistics about agriculture, wages, industry and health care. But there was never any mention of spiritual needs. There seemed to be total governmental ignorance to the fact of what the Bible and Watchman Nee so clearly taught: that man is a three-part being: spirit, soul and body. The assumption was that all needs were being met by the state, a totally materialistic view, of course. But did not the greatest of proletariats — Jesus — insist that man should not live by bread alone but by every word that proceeds out of God's mouth?

Down a fetid alley in the communal home of an old woman, I decided to make my point. Our hostess served tea on an overturned wooden crate. Flies competed with us for the bowl of biscuits. The floor was dirt, the room was filled with debris and farm equipment. A wall clock and a portrait of Mao were the only modern accoutrements.

During a question and answer period, I purposely asked the old woman, through our young translator, about provision for spiritual concerns. But the translator never directed the question to the old woman. Instead, she answered it herself by saying: "God is the old way. We have new way now."

Some church officials in the West deny that Christianity is still alive in China. Others say they have evidence that the underground church (not the official showcase churches) is indeed alive. There is a considerable body of evidence about small group activities of the underground church that filters through in testimonies in letters and through those Chinese who have managed passage to Hong Kong. Mary Wang, for example, author of *The Chinese Church that Will Not Die*, testifies that a letter from a labour camp reads: "Pray for us. We are in Gethsemane and near to Calvary."

The Most Rev. Donald Coggan, former Archbishop of Canterbury, has said that Western Christians should intercede for the underground church. He rightly asserted that the blood of the martyrs has been the seed of a persecuted but vital church behind the Bamboo Curtain. Testimonies in Christian journals have described some young people who were brought up under the atheistic regime who nevertheless have embraced Christianity. Some estimate there are as many as one million secret believers in China. But only God knows for sure how many believers there are. Now that China is open to the West, there are reports that Chinese Christians are becoming more bold. Gospel radio broadcasts from Taiwan into the mainland, for example, have produced many grateful letters. Even the government has been known to accept the lucrative offers of American TV evangelists to air their Gospel messages.

During the next decade, China plans to become a major industrial power. And the fact that one-fourth of the world's population is subjected to such a complete national discipline is one of the most awesome developments in the history of man.

What does this mean for the Gospel? God is still exercising his sovereignty over the affairs and nations of men, even the giant People's Republic of China. God, in his Providence, has permitted this system temporarily, much as he prepared the Roman Empire as a vehicle through which Christianity was originally spread.

After all, hasn't China been purged of all pagan religions as well? And doesn't every family now own a radio set to receive communist messages? Can't these same radios be used to receive Christian broadcasts beamed into the mainland from Manila, Hong Kong or Taiwan? Haven't roads been built to the remotest Chinese villages, enhancing communications? And hasn't the language been simplified so that peasant folk can now read, and therefore read the Bible some day, too?

God will eventually overturn this evil regime and use its very machinery for his own divine purposes to reach the Chinese people. There have been three great attempts by missionaries in the past to evangelise China. The way for a fourth, ever greater and far-reaching one, has already been paved.

Chapter 8

Hong Kong

China was behind us now. Back in Hong Kong, we were to sail at midnight, but first Peter went to the Cable and Wireless Office to send a message to my parents in Virginia.

"Went fishing in Canton. Everything okay," the telegram read, assuring parents anxious about the Bibles that we had indeed been Christian 'fishermen' in China but were now safely back across the border.

Meanwhile, I had walked the short distance from the Ocean Terminal to the Hong Kong YMCA. In my purse was a Chinese Bible held in reserve for Dr. Wang, and I hoped to stumble upon someone at the YMCA who could help me to mail it to him properly. I remembered the warning of a former Presbyterian missionary to China, my good friend Sallie Reed, that for a Chinese person to receive mail from a Westerner could put him under suspicion. I asked the YMCA receptionist if there were any evangelicals there who could help me.

"I suppose you should see Mr. Lee," she suggested. "He's usually up on the roof garden every evening reading his Bible. Take the elevator up."

I entered the elevator and pushed the 'R' for roof garden. The automatic door opened to a magnificent panorama of Hong Kong bespangled with brilliant white lights, fluorescent greens and neon reds.

I assumed I was looking for a Chinaman. But the gentleman sitting at a table, sipping tea and perusing his Bible was an Englishman — Mr. A.T. Lee.

"Pardon me," I said, "are you Mr. Lee?"

"I am," he said, standing up cordially.

"I was told by the front desk that you're an evangelical and the most likely person to be able to help me."

"Well, praise the Lord," Mr. Lee, a man in his 60s, laughed jovially. "What can I do for you?"

He offered me a seat.

"My husband and I are passengers on the Queen Elizabeth 2, which sails in a few hours tonight, and we don't want to leave Hong Kong with this Chinese Bible in our possession . . ."

Before I could say more, Mr. Lee interrupted me, enthusing: "This is amazing! You've come to the right place. The man who is a close friend of the person who prints these Bibles is standing right over there!"

Mr. Lee pointed to an American who was taking some time exposures of the panorama with his camera. "Pastor Keener!" he called. "Come over here and meet this lady."

Pastor Keener, an Assemblies of God minister, joined us at the rooftop table. I related my story more fully about our 'chance' encounter with Dr. Wang in Canton. I lamented that Peter and I had not given him a Bible.

"I even have his address. Just think," I winced, "he could be reading this Bible right now."

"I can assist you in getting it to him," Mr. Lee said with an adventurous twinkle in his eyes.

"You can?" I exclaimed joyfully. "How?"

"My dear," the Englishman explained, "I have lived here so many years that I write Chinese very well. I can package this Bible anonymously, address it in Chinese to your Dr. Wang and it will get through. Much mail is exchanged between Hong Kong and China. But if you try to address it to him, the package will look suspect."

Gladly, I gave the remaining New Testament to Mr. Lee along with Dr. Wang's address. He immediately translated it into fine Chinese characters. (A letter I received months later from Mr. Lee reported that the Bible did eventually reach Canton through the hands of some Chinese friends.) Then for a while the three of us shared our common faith.

"Mr. Lee knows a lot of influential people in Hong Kong, and he was instrumental in setting up my ministry here," Pastor Keener related. "I represent the International Hotel Ministries over there in the Furama Intercontinental Hotel." He pointed out a posh, 32-storey hotel on the skyline of Hong Kong Island. "God gave me a definite call to come out here to minister to the educated, English-speaking community of this city, since there were already plenty of missionaries to the Chinese residents. Through Mr. Lee and his business contacts, we were able to establish regular transdenominational worship services in the hotel's Jade Ballroom. The hotel furnishes everything, including the piano, the organ and the chairs. There's no overhead. It's truly a work of the Holy Spirit.

"We're reaching the unchurched people of many nationalities who pass through here," he continued. "Many of these people would never step inside a traditional worship service, but they will attend ours in a hotel. We've led Buddhists, Hindus and persons of many faiths to Jesus. On any given Sunday, we see Chinese, Ceylonese, Indonesians, Filipinos, Indians, Americans, Australians, Japanese and Malaysians all worshipping together. It's truly beautiful."

Mr. Lee, the internal auditor of a branch of European banks in Hong Kong, said he had been a Christian only a few years, but the Lord had completely transformed his life.

"I was born and brought up a 'normal Anglican'. That means I went to church on special occasions — weddings and funerals! It took me 60 years to find the truth.

"Through various circumstances, my family was led to New Zealand, because it was there that my younger son found the Lord. His strange behaviour and change of character led my wife to inquire and eventually to walk that same path. I went to Auckland to straighten them out from this fanaticism, and I ended up back in Hong Kong filled with the Holy Spirit!

"Before that wonderful day in Auckland, I subscribed to a sort of belief in evolution, and I was sympathetic toward Islam, Buddhism and Confucianism. God certainly had to deal with much in my life." He threw back his head with a good-natured laugh, adding: "I don't mind telling you that for two months I suffered the mental tortures of Hell. The devil was on my trail. He was furious because of what happened in Auckland. And he wasted no time in trying to make me turn back again to my old ways."

"What happened?" I asked, almost forgetting that it was nigh time for me to return to the ship.

"I would wake up at night and again in the mornings filled with a black sense of impending disaster. I was engulfed in mental depression. A doctor friend said I should go to a mental home before he was compelled to send me there! He prescribed tranquillisers. The manager of my bank, an old friend, later told me that he was about to release me from my duties.

"But my newly found Christian friends rallied around me and were wonderfully supportive. Pastors suspected that the devil was making a last-ditch effort to retrieve me. They consoled me with Scriptures.

"There was one verse that I particularly clung to, 1 Corinthians 10: 13, 'There hath no temptation taken you but such as is common to man: but God is faithful, who will not suffer you to be tempted above that ye are able; but will with the temptation also make a way to escape, that ye may be able to bear it.'

"Praise the Lord! I kept clinging to that verse, and one day the darkness just lifted. It was a battle, but Jesus delivered me. All my burdens rolled away, and they haven't been back since."

I regretfully glanced at my watch again. My new friends promised to pray for me that week in their hotel meeting.

"Oh," I added, as I stood up to leave, "please pray for a waiter who has just rejoined the ship. He's very open to Jesus. His name is Jonathan Saunders."

"We claim Jonathan Saunders in the Name of Jesus!" Pastor Keener shouted with authority, as if his very words were loosening something in the heavenlies.

"I wish you could talk to him." I was clearly awed with the power of the Holy Spirit in the lives of these two men. "I don't think I've ever led anyone to the Lord before."

"What you need is the Baptism in the Holy Spirit," Pastor Keener said, giving a knowing look to Mr. Lee. "We'll pray for that to happen, too."

☆ ☆ ☆

The QE2's midnight departure was a spectacle. A crowd had gathered at the Ocean Terminal to watch the ship sail. Passengers sang giddily 'Auld Lang Syne' to the music of a military band on the quay. Paper streamers streaked through the air. The ship's pipes blew a long, mellow blast, causing pulses to quicken. Then the ship slowly began to slide away from the dock. Some passengers cried as they waved to friends.

Others were boisterous with drink. I gazed at the roof garden of the YMCA one last time, musing upon my 'chance' meeting with Mr. Lee and Pastor Keener.

"What you need is the Baptism in the Holy Spirit . . ." His words echoed in my ears. He was talking about the Pentecostal experience, but I was the daughter of a conservative Presbyterian minister. My husband was also graduated from a Presbyterian seminary and was an officer in the Presbyterian church. Yet, I felt so powerless. Inwardly, I knew Pastor Keener was right. I was afraid, though. Suppose I didn't receive the Holy Spirit, but some deceptive spirit? And those tongues that were supposed to come with the Baptism of the Holy Spirit. How would I know they weren't just gibberish?

Burt Singer, a Jewish boxer-turned-believer in Jesus, once told me that he never prayed for persons to receive the Baptism in the Holy Spirit unless they were desperate for it.

"God doesn't honour the casual inquirer," Burt said. "I only pray for the desperate ones. I tell the casual inquirers to simmer on the back burner until they're desperate for the power of God."

I was still apprehensive. But I was also getting desperate.

Back in my cabin, I opened my Bible, looking for a verse that would give me some sort of direction or comfort in my dilemma. The verses where my eyes fell seemed to answer all my apprehensions about the Baptism of the Holy Spirit:

"If a son shall ask bread of any of you that is a father, will he give him a stone? or if he ask a fish, will he for a fish give him a serpent? Or if he shall ask an egg, will he offer him a scorpion? If you then, being evil, know how to give good gifts unto your children: how much more shall your heavenly Father give the Holy Spirit to them that ask him?" *Luke 11: 11—13*

Chapter 9

Fire at Sea

March 16 was both a dark night of the soul and a great day of rejoicing. It was the international date-line day, a Wednesday, which we had the curious experience of living twice in the Pacific Ocean. Somewhere near the imaginary meridian, there were two March 16ths. Like the jubilant Phileas Fogg in Jules Verne's *Around the World in Eighty Days*, who discovered that he had an extra golden day, we were to reclaim the 24 hours we had lost going east through various time zones.

After the first Wednesday, we were given the peculiar bonus of a 24-hour repeat, but this time with different menus in the restaurant, an 'international date-line edition' of the 'QE2 Times' and a completely new agenda of activities.

"Think of the people who'd give anything to live a day over again," Peter remarked at breakfast. "Well, we're going to have that opportunity!"

But as we sailed toward Hawaii on that first Wednesday, I began to sense the end of the voyage drawing near for us, coupled with an overwhelming grief (or was it frustration?) at the powerlessness I felt as a believer. Suddenly, the accumulation of nearly three months of emotions inundated me as I recalled the poverty among the shantytowns of South America; the cancerous atmosphere of despair building in South Africa; the doleful hovels and begging faces of India; and the ever-present occult spreading its roots deep into the cultures of so many peoples.

Until this trip, I simply had not realised that much of the world's population is still blindly bound into worshipping cattle and monkeys and snakes. In sophisticated Japan, the electronics hub of the world, some of the most grotesque idols in Kyoto were glaring shadows of the images of Hell. During an excursion from Tokyo to Kyoto, we visited temples whose idols would have given me nightmares as a child. One in particular, carved of wood, appeared to be about 20 feet high and glared down at me with a ferocity that was chilling. Another wooden idol outside that temple was dressed in a red cape and white cap like Little Red Riding Hood, but the face was more evil than the proverbial wolf.

The inflamed face of a little ragged girl back in Bali would keep reappearing in my mind. She had accosted us for alms at the quayside and was a marred memory of that near Edenic isle. My impulse had been to reach out and pray for her healing in the Name of Jesus, just as the apostles would have done in the Bible, but I resisted because of fear . . . and powerlessness. Yet, unquestionably, Jesus, Peter, John and Paul would have touched her and made her whole. My Lord had promised that certain signs would follow believers: we were to cast out demons, lay hands on the sick and also speak in new tongues. So why was I spiritually paralysed?

I felt such a burden for nations and for individual souls, such as Professor Vishnu back in Bombay, that after dinner I could only think of retreating from everything. In the solitude of Deck Five, while most of the passengers were partying as usual in the ship's night clubs and cocktail bars far above me, I quietly began to seek God.

Coupled with my own feelings of inadequacy as a believer, I was incredibly thirsty for the Spirit of God. I lacked power. It was agonising! I lamented, like the

St. Mary — ON THE ROCK
Family Communion/Sunday School/Creche
ST. PETER — TORRY
Holy Communion   8.30 a.m. (1st Sunday Only)
Sung Eucharist   11.15 a.m.

39 Pentecostal

NEW HOPE CHRISTIAN CENTRE

FAITH ACRES, PETERHEAD

Tel 0779 838251

ONE NIGHT ONLY!

Special visit of Rodney Howard Browne

South African Evangelist and Revivalist,

Friday, July 9, at 7 p.m.

Fresh from an outstanding revival in Carpenters Home Church, Orlando, Florida, 6,000 Converts in six weeks, 2,000 baptized in water in one 4hr. service! This is a Revival, unique manifestations of the power of God in every meeting.

Don't miss this opportunity! If you're hungry, This is bread!

If your life needs reviving, This is revival!

EVERYONE WELCOME.

50 Other Services

balance presentation of
...ening primrose oil and fish oil.
...e Callanish range - for the
maintainence of good health.

EVENING PRIMROSE OIL MARINE 50 OMEGA COMBINATION
EVENING PRIMROSE OIL MARINE 50 OMEGA COMBINATION
EVENING PRIMROSE OIL MARINE 50 OMEGA COMBINATION
EVENING PRIMROSE OIL MARINE 50 OMEGA COMBINATION
EVENING PRIMROSE OIL MARINE 50 OMEGA COMBINATION
EVENING PRIMROSE OIL MARINE 50 OMEGA COMBINATION
EVENING PRIMROSE OIL MARINE 50 OMEGA COMBINATION
EVENING PRIMROSE OIL MARINE 50 OMEGA COMBINATION
EVENING PRIMROSE OIL MARINE 50 OMEGA COMBINATION
EVENING PRIMROSE OIL MARINE 50 OMEGA COMBINATION

20p OFF

WHEN YOU PURCHASE ANY OF THE ABOVE CALLANISH PRODUCTS

INVERNESS
Baron Taylor Lane • Wee Health Shop, Market
...uthside Road • J C Cameron, 8 Greig
...reet • J R Henderson

Ancient Mariner: "Water, water everywhere, nor any drop to drink!" Yet Jesus had promised: "If anyone is thirsty, let him come to me, and drink. He that believes on me . . . out of his innermost being shall flow rivers of living water."

For a long while I lay on my berth reducing tissues to wet shreds and thinking this was an unusual way to spend time on a world cruise. It didn't seem to affect Peter as deeply; he was enjoying a film in the ship's theatre and wouldn't be back for several hours.

I stared at the cabin's white ceiling. Beyond the port-hole, the black waves of the Pacific hissed away from the bow, and the dried salt spray seemed to imitate tear streaks on the glass. I suddenly had the thought that wherever we went on this journey, Jesus had already been there establishing his church. Yet I could sense the Spirit's wrestling with the powers of darkness, and for just a moment, I felt the powers of darkness were winning.

Hoping for some comfort or guidance, I picked up my Bible from the dresser. It fell open to Psalm 77:

> I cry aloud to God,
> aloud to God, that he may hear me.
> In the day of my trouble I seek the Lord;
> . . . my soul refuses to be comforted.
> I think of God, and I moan;
> I meditate, and my spirit faints . . .
> Thou dost hold my eyelids from closing;
> I am so troubled that I cannot speak . . .

This psalm seemed to epitomise my despair at the unevangelised state of the world and my own powerlessness. News from America showed that it was becoming more anti-Christian. An issue of *Time Magazine* that we picked up in Japan gave yet another quote from a White House official who carelessly blasphemed God's name.

Through the gift of travel, I had been given a vision of a world so corrupt, that it seemed impossible for anyone to have faith, or for me to affect my world for good. I continued to read Psalm 77:

> I meditate and search my spirit:
> "Will the Lord spurn forever,
> and never again be favourable?
> Has his steadfast love forever ceased?
> Are his promises at an end for all time?
> Has God forgotten to be gracious?
> Has he in anger shut up his compassion?"

Yet somehow I sensed a deep inner conviction that all this soul-searching was about to accomplish a break-through in my life. For I was soon to realise that when a person is really in the depths of spiritual need, God is ready to console with his power.

I remembered a verse in Luke 24:49, which promises very definite power for service after Jesus gave his commission to go into all the world: "And behold, I send the promise of my Father upon you: but tarry . . . until ye be endued with power from on high."

I was determined to tarry, to wait, in my cabin all evening until I received this power from on high.

"If Jesus commanded his disciples not to work without it," I said aloud, "then I, as one of his disciples, will not presume to live another day without it!"

Among my bedside papers was a sermon by Billy Graham. It was entitled *The Fire of God*, in which he stated that without the fire of God he would never dare to preach. Upon reading this, I confessed every sin I could think of (for I intuitively knew that Jesus will not fill an unclean vessel). Then, quite spontaneously, because I now had a clear conscience toward God, I began to cry out boldly: "Let the fire fall!"

I don't recall how long I did this, but the Holy Spirit began to saturate my darkened cabin with ocean waves of His presence. His manifestation literally engulfed me with a wave of powerful joy. Breakers of joy that would register number 10 on a 'spiritual Richter scale' ebbed and rolled over my spirit. This joy was so different from its regular human counterpart that I felt this must be what the atmosphere of heaven is like. I didn't want this spirit baptism to end, but I simply could not bear any longer the weight of God's power in that measure of intensity.

However, there was nothing frightening about the Baptism in the Holy Spirit, as I once, in my ignorance, had imagined. Rather, this joyous overshadowing was scriptural, as Psalm 16:11 says: ". . . in thy presence is fullness of joy . . .". In fact, in Acts Chapter 2, when the disciples in the Upper Room were filled with the Holy Spirit, they were so joyous that mockers accused them of being drunk on new wine!

Interestingly, at the same time that my spirit was being immersed in the Holy Spirit, I felt welling up from within my innermost being mysterious words that wanted to gush forth like water breaking over a dam. Intuitively, I knew these words were in adoration of God. But I also sensed that I was in full control of my faculties and could stop the words from being spoken, if I so desired. By an act of my will, I could turn off the flow as easily as a faucet is controlled by a tap. (That is why 1 Corinthians 14:32 clearly says "the spirits of prophets are subject to the prophets.")

My spirit enjoyed the liberty released by a new prayer language. I felt as if my capacity to express myself before God had increased. It was a boost in vocabulary. But my mind objected. Let me say here very carefully that in spiritual matters, the mind is absolutely essential, but the mind must learn to be dominated by man's immortal spirit and not the spirit dominated by the mind. Only the spiritual man discerns spiritual things, and the natural man therefore does not receive the things of the Spirit of God (*1 Corinthians 2:14*).

So my mind stood aloof, like a reporter, taking notes. I could actually see myself in my mind's eye with my familiar reporter's notebook, jotting down observations: "Oh, no! I can't believe this is really happening. I'm going to speak in tongues! It's not rational."

Meanwhile, my immortal spirit, which is an entirely separate organism from my mind, conversely argued: "It is written, 'Those who hunger and thirst after righteousness shall be filled!' It is also written that one who speaks in an unknown tongue utters mysteries in the Spirit and edifies himself."

The mind can be renewed by the washing of the Word in order to agree with what the spirit of man knows to be true. So that night in cabin 5069, I finally received the imbuement of power that the Apostle Peter said was promised "unto you, and to your children, and to all that are afar off, even as many as the Lord our God shall call (*Acts 2:39*)."

I knew that I was, at last, empowered to win souls.

☆   ☆   ☆

Somewhere in the twilight zone of early morning, I received a dream from God. I was back in my childhood home. Everything in the home, including myself, my family, the furniture, even the telephone, was ablaze with forked tongues of fire, but nothing was being consumed. This was similar to the apostles' experience on the day of Pentecost when the Holy Spirit came like a mighty rushing wind and alighted upon them in the form of lambent, cloven flames. In the dream, I ran out of my house yelling: "Fire! Fire!" with such intensity that I awakened instantly. As I sat up in my berth, I knew that I must read Matthew 3:11.

I didn't have a clue what that verse said. But there was an inner prompting to read Matthew 3:11. I quickly turned to it:

"I indeed baptise you with water unto repentance: but he that comes after me is mightier than I, whose shoes I am not worthy to bear: *he shall baptise you with the Holy Ghost, and with fire . . .*"

The dream was a confirmation that I had truly been baptised with the Holy Spirit . . . *and fire*. That verse is very significant. Many people claim to have the Holy Spirit, but if there is no fire in their lives — no zeal — then something is seriously wrong.

March 16 on the international date-line had begun in despair; now it had dawned again with new hope, just as the overwhelmed writer of Psalm 77 received new power:

> . . . And I say, "It is my grief that the
> right hand of the Most High has changed."
> I will call to mind the deeds of the Lord;
> yea, I will remember thy wonders of old.
> I will meditate on all thy work,
> and muse on thy mighty deeds.
> Thy way, O God, is holy.
> What god is great like our God?
> Thou art the God who workest wonders . . .
>
> When the waters saw thee, O God,
> When the waters saw thee,
> they were afraid,
> yea, the deep trembled . . .
>
> Thy way was through the sea,
> thy path through the great waters . . .

Chapter 10

Fishing for Men

The evening of the second 'international Wednesday', Peter agreed that we should invite Jonathan Saunders to our cabin after he had finished working. Jonathan had been asking so many questions about Jesus that we knew he was ready to have the Gospel explained to him.

At about 11p.m., there was a knock on the door. Jonathan's red jacket was removed and the sleeves of his starched white shirt were rolled up. We offered him a seat on Peter's berth and some pillows to lean on. His black curly head rested against the wall under the porthole. The red curtains swayed with the rolling of the ship, and occasional sudsy waves washed over the glass.

It was just the three of us, below in the Five Deck cabin on a ship of lights sailing in the darkness, God only knew where, talking about eternal things while dice rolled in the casino above and couples danced the night away.

We asked the night steward for a pot of tea and talked for a good while about the East End of London, where Jonathan's family lives. But Jonathan was a seeker, and the conversation turned to the inevitable: What is truth? Is it possible to be saved?

We asked Jonathan if he had come to the point in his spiritual life that if he were to die tonight, did he have any assurance that he would inherit eternal life? Jonathan's ever-present smile showed a hint of embarrassment. He crossed his arms defensively across his chest and shrugged his shoulders with a laugh.

"I don't know. I've done a lot of things in my life."

"But you can be forgiven for everything," I said to encourage him.

"Well, let's look at it this way," Peter said, sitting up straight. His green eyes were bright with the challenge. "Suppose you were to die tonight and you found yourself before God, and he asked you: 'Why do you deserve heaven?' What answer would you give?"

Jonathan looked down at the floor, his arms still crossed.

"Aven't got a clue," he said. His accent was somewhat cockneyish, but also lacked a strong regional ring, since he had lived half his life at sea.

"But suppose you had to give some answer," I added, knowing that his answer would reveal what he was trusting in.

Jonathan looked up, threw his arms out playfully, as if he were entreating God: "Well, come on, Chief, have a heart and please let me in."

At that, all three of us broke out in laughter. Jonathan grinned broadly, and we felt the love of God for him. It was such a winsome remark, even if it wasn't the Biblical answer God is looking for. At least Jonathan didn't offer the usual self-righteous answers people might give to that question, such as: "I deserve heaven because I've lived a good life," or, "I've kept the Ten Commandments," or, "Well, I've never harmed anybody."

Jonathan knew he hadn't lived a perfect life, that there were things in his past for which he would have to give an accounting. We told him the good news that the 'Chief' did, in fact, have a heart in providing a substitute, his own Son, to pay for our sins on the cross so that we could have free entry to heaven. We showed him the various Scriptures in the book of Romans where it states that all have sinned and fallen short of the mark and that someone, namely Jesus, took the rap for us.

"How do we know that God's anger against our sin was satisfied when Jesus was punished in our place?" I interjected. "Because God didn't leave Jesus in the grave to rot. He raised Him from the dead. Jesus was declared to be the Son of God with power through the Resurrection."

Jonathan's face looked troubled. He lowered his head again, and all I could see now was the black top of his thick hair.

"Jonathan," I continued, "we're journalists, we're broadcasters. As a journalist, I know for a fact that the Resurrection of Jesus really happened. I know it not only because I know Him personally and that He's alive, but also because the New Testament is factual, journalistic accounts written by eye witnesses."

I showed him 2 Peter 1:16, where Simon Peter said the disciples did not follow 'cleverly devised myths' but instead were 'eyewitnesses of his majesty.'

"According to Hebrew law," I continued, "the testimony of two witnesses in court was considered valid. Yet we are told in the New Testament that Jesus appeared not only to His disciples, but also to a crowd of 500 persons at once. Now that kind of evidence for the Resurrection would have to hold up in court!"

It was nearly midnight and the ship began to roll, pitch and groan, but Jonathan was alert and interested. He unfolded his arms. His brown eyes squinted keenly.

"Yes, but, if all this is true about Jesus, how come nobody has ever come back from the spirit world to tell us about it?"

My heart jumped. "Show him the parable about the man named Lazarus!" I enthused to Peter.

"Yes," Peter said with his customary calmness.

"There is a story in the New Testament that answers that very question."

"Here it is!" I exclaimed excitedly as I found 'Lazarus' in my concordance. "It's in Luke, Chapter 16."

'There was a rich man, who was clothed in purple and fine linen and who feasted sumptuously every day. And at his gate lay a poor man named Lazarus, full of sores, who desired to be fed with what fell from the rich man's table . . . The poor man died and was carried by the angels to Abraham's bosom. The rich man also died and was buried; and in Hades, being in torment, he lifted up his eyes and saw Abraham far off and Lazarus in his bosom.'

'And he cried out: "Father, Abraham, have mercy upon me, and send Lazarus to dip the end of his finger in water and cool my tongue; for I am in anguish in this flame".'

"The story goes on to say that Lazarus couldn't do anything to help the rich man in Hell because between them was fixed a great gulf that no one could cross.

"Next, the former rich man begs Abraham to send Lazarus back to warn his five brothers not to come to such a place of torment. But listen to Abraham's sobering answer," I urged, looking up at Jonathan. 'If they do not hear Moses and the prophets, neither will they be convinced if some one should rise from the dead.'

We were all silent for a moment. Then Peter said: "See, this is describing exactly what you were asking about. You wanted someone to come back from the dead to convince you that there is a heaven and a hell and a Saviour, and here Jesus is warning you that you must have faith in his word. He has given you everything you need to know how to have salvation in this book. So you don't need someone from the spirit world to convince you."

Jonathan shook his head affirmatively and seemed satisfied with this answer. I couldn't stand the suspense any longer. I popped the question.

"Jonathan, tonight you could ask Jesus to come into your life and transform it. God could use you mightily on this ship. Wouldn't you like to receive Jesus?"

"Perhaps I should go back to my cabin and think about it," he said pensively.

"But now is the day of salvation," I pressed, not willing to give up.

I felt led to share with him the doctrine of Jesus' Second Coming and how, according to the prophecies, his coming is imminent. We pointed out some of the major prophecies of Jesus' return in Matthew 24 and Luke 21, especially the restoration of the Jews to the Holy Land and their recapture of East Jerusalem in 1967.

The fulfilled prophecies stirred Jonathan's interest and seemed to convince him more than anything of the veracity of God's Word. A reverential fear of God came upon him. We asked him a second time if he'd like to give his life to Jesus.

"Yes," Jonathan said, with a smile of relief coming out like sunshine from behind a cloud of uncertainty.

"Wow! You really mean it?" Peter and I chorused.

"Yes, I really mean it."

The three of us held hands across the two berths and Jonathan asked Jesus to forgive him, to come into his life and to direct him.

☆ ☆ ☆

In the morning as we ascended the five decks to breakfast, I was a bit apprehensive about seeing Jonathan. I was worried whether or not the previous night's experience had 'taken'.

But Jonathan's disposition was sunny, and he was glad to see us. We asked Oliver and Charlie for tea and toast and talked to Jonathan as he set the table next to us. Jay and Tiffany had come and gone an hour earlier.

"I really took a ribbing this morning," Jonathan said. "I was reading the Bible you gave me, and the room steward came in and said: 'What you reading? The Bible!' He was trying to take the mickey out of me. I said: 'Yeah, it makes good reading.'"

Something sank within me. I knew what he was going to be up against.

"Word travels fast," Jonathan continued. "Several of the boys were knocking on my door and making jokes."

I attempted some word of encouragement.

"Oh, it doesn't bother me," Jonathan said confidently. "What went on in my cabin this morning was nothing compared to what Jesus went through."

I smiled a relieved smile as we headed for the morning's lecture on Hawaii.

"Have a good morning, madam," Jonathan called after me.

"I will if you don't call me madam anymore!" I said. "You're my brother now!"

☆ ☆ ☆

At lunchtime, Oliver and Charlie were visibly piqued at the attention Jonathan was getting. He must have shared with them what had happened the night before, because they were ribbing him, too.

"So he thinks he's got religion, does he?" Charlie smiled sarcastically. "Well, he's got a lot of changing to do before he'll convince me."

Along with Jay and Tiffany, we were sharing an order of macaroni — not the usual fare on a world cruise — but Tiffany had been craving her favourite dish for weeks. Afterwards, Peter and I lingered over our coffee. Buoyant from our experience with Jonathan, we now had the courage to ask Oliver and Charlie down to our cabin to tell them about Jesus.

"Sure," they both said, when we invited them. They seemed pleased. We asked Jonathan to come along, too.

"Honey, I know something wonderful is going to happen again tonight. I just know it!" I said to Peter late that afternoon on the Lido Deck. He was tuning in his shortwave radio to the American Forces Network. Hawaii was only a day away.

At about 11p.m., Oliver and Charlie arrived at our door. We offered them seats on the berths. Charlie took the dresser stool.

"Allow us to wait on you for a change," Peter said, ceremoniously folding a bath towel over his arm to imitate a waiter's tea towel.

"We don't drink," Charlie said, pulling out his cigarettes. "Just order us some Cokes, please."

We began to talk about ship life. Oliver and Charlie were interesting characters, and they entertained us with stories about passengers' jewels and stowaways.

"Do you know," Charlie said, "there's a safe on this ship filled with jewels that were left in various cabins? There's no way a woman is ever going to claim them."

"Why not?" I asked naively.

"Because," Charlie smiled mischievously and took a drag on his cigarette, "to claim them is to admit they were carousing in the cabin of somebody who's not exactly their husband."

"Oh, you're joking," I said.

"Honest." Charlie said. "That's the honest truth." He flicked some ashes into the tray. The cabin was beginning to fill up with smoke.

Peter asked about the stowaways.

"I remember one time a whole family got on in South Africa," Oliver said. "After the ship was at sea, they confessed. They were fined, of course."

"The most brazen one," Charlie piped in, "was the man who was caught because he didn't like the people at his dinner table. Imagine that. When he had the cheek to ask for another table, the head waiter discovered that the man didn't even have a cabin."

"Then," Oliver said, "there was the stowaway who went through an entire voyage without being caught until he boasted to somebody in a Southampton shop. The braggart was apprehended before he could leave town."

Jonathan popped in and sat down on one of the berths. He hardly entered into the conversation. Instead, he was absorbed in reading the *Good News* Bible, occasionally exclaiming: "Look at this! I never knew the Bible said this. This is fantastic!"

The Bible fell open to the book of Proverbs. "Listen to this," Jonathan interrupted, pointing to Proverbs 23: 29–34:

"Show me someone who drinks too much, who has to try out fancy drinks, and I will show you someone miserable and sorry for himself, always causing trouble and always complaining. His eyes are bloodshot, and he has bruises that could have been avoided. Don't let wine tempt you even though it is rich red, and it sparkles in the cup, and it goes down smoothly. The next morning you will feel as if you had been bitten by a poisonous snake. Weird sights will appear before your eyes, and you will not be able to think or speak clearly. You will feel as if you were out on the ocean seasick, swinging high up in the rigging of a tossing ship."

"Isn't that incredibly appropriate?" Jonathan asked. Then he mused to himself: "Every time I pick up the

Bible, it falls open to something meaningful."

Our attention turned again to Oliver and Charlie. Peter asked them the two leading questions that have been so effective in Florida's Coral Ridge Presbyterian Church's 'Evangelism Explosion' — 'Have you come to a point in your spiritual life that if you were to die tonight you're sure that you'll go to heaven?' and, 'If you were to die tonight and found yourself before God, what reason would you offer him for allowing you into heaven?' The questions are posed to determine who or what the person is trusting in for eternal life: his own 'good works', or perhaps a religious system.

Both their answers indicated that they were not trusting in the atoning work of Jesus Christ on the cross. Oliver had been reared, like so many British children, in the Church of England, but he still did not know the Gospel that we are saved by faith in Jesus Christ. Charlie, on the other hand, had heard more than enough about 'religion' from his wife, a Jehovah's Witness.

We explained the Gospel again of Jesus' substitutionary death for our sins and also showed Charlie how the Jehovah's Witnesses are a zealous end-time false cult, just as Jesus had predicted for the last days.

"God so loved you, Oliver and Charlie," I said earnestly, "that he gave his only begotten Son that whosoever believes in Him will have eternal life." Inwardly, I was freshly amazed at the simplicity of the Gospel and how easy it is to communicate.

Oliver sat silently. The Spirit of God was upon him. Always the Spirit of God is upon those who are hearing the Gospel. I told him it was no accident that God had seated us at his table, that God was striving very hard to save his soul.

"Yes, I can tell. He's striving to reach me through you," Oliver said seriously. There was no trace in his voice of his usual jesting.

"Do I have to give up smoking?" Oliver asked in a childlike manner.

"God may convict you of that," Peter said, "but the important thing tonight is that you come into a personal relationship with his Son."

Then Oliver said he wanted to be sure that he was saved. He said he wanted to pray to receive Jesus into his heart! Meanwhile, the Spirit of God was softening Charlie. He was in no hurry to leave. But he could not bring himself to make a commitment.

"Don't get me wrong," Charlie apologised, "I've enjoyed this very much. I really have. But I just don't feel nothing inside." He shrugged his stocky shoulders. "I can't accept Jesus, not tonight, anyway."

"Charlie, never depend on feelings," I exhorted. "Feelings can deceive us. Go on the facts about what the Bible teaches. You need Jesus."

Jonathan looked up from perusing the Bible to concur. "If you won't receive Jesus now, would you at least let us pray for you?" I asked, taking his hand. There seemed to be something healing in a gentle touch.

"Sure," Charlie said agreeably. "I wouldn't mind that at all."

This time all five of us held hands around the berths as Peter first led Oliver in a prayer of repentance and receiving Jesus, and then a prayer claiming Charlie for Christ until he can believe on his own.

Something was happening to Charlie. Tears were running down the cheeks of this man who had snarled at me weeks earlier with his fist balled up: "Don't tell me about God!"

After Peter prayed, Charlie wiped his eyes unabashedly.

"That was the most beautiful prayer I've ever heard. I could have listened all night."

98

Charlie had opened a crack in the door of his heart for the Holy Spirit to begin a work. God knew it. And Charlie knew it. Meanwhile, we were ecstatic over Oliver's response to the sinner's prayer.

"When I was just a lad," Oliver said, "I used to ride my bicycle every Sunday over to the village church. I remember one time, during a church pageant, I was one of the S's."

"What do you mean?" I asked.

"The children held up posters that spelled: 'Jesus Saves.' I was one of the S's."

There was a pregnant silence in the cabin for a moment. We were all touched by the simplicity of Oliver's childhood recollection, and the sovereignty of God in his life. God had not forgotten Oliver.

"I've wandered a long way from the fold," he said. "But I'm back in now."

☆ ☆ ☆

As they left, Oliver shook everybody's hand, kissed me on the cheek and called me his sister. Charlie said wistfully, pointing at Oliver: "I hope you know, you've caught a big one."

Chapter 11

Jonathan

The ship was docked overnight in Hawaii. Peter, Jay, Tiffany and I agreed to meet Jonathan after the restaurant was deserted to watch his portable TV. It was the first time we'd seen American television in nearly three months, but we soon realised it had been no great loss. Jay and Tiffany eventually wandered off to the dance floor and Peter said he had some reading to catch up on. Jonathan and I remained talking in the restaurant while some of his mates watched the portable TV.

"I have a confession," Jonathan said, somewhat apprehensively. "I lied when I told you I was from Malta."

I quickly assessed his features. He certainly could have passed for a native from that small Mediterranean island. His skin was olive; his eyes dark brown.

"What difference does it make where you're from?" I asked.

"Ever heard of the Copts?" he queried.

"Sure. They're Egyptian Christians."

"Well, my mother is pure Egyptian — not an Arab, mind you." He lowered his voice. "My mother was a descendant of those original Egyptian Christians. There's a world of difference between them and the Moslem Arabs."

"It's really beautiful, Jonathan," I said excitedly, marvelling that the first person we'd led to the Lord had a Middle Eastern background. "You should be proud of your roots, especially in light of the news today and Bible prophecies."

He quickly shushed me.

"I don't want anybody on this ship to know I'm half Egyptian . . . 'specially them." He motioned toward some of his mates, but they were absorbed in the TV programme.

"Why?" I insisted. "You should be proud of your heritage." I reached in my purse for my Bible and showed him the prophecy in Isaiah 19:25 foretelling a future time of peace when the Lord will ultimately declare:

"Blessed be Egypt my people, and Assyria the work of my hands, and Israel my heritage."

Jonathan looked pleased. It was the first time anybody had ever said anything positive about his Egyptian blood.

"You wouldn't believe the number of times I've gotten into fights because somebody thought I'm an Arab."

"I can imagine," I said, "because the Arabs are also Semites, you know. They suffer from anti-Semitism, too."

"I've been hit too many times and hated just because I look like an Arab. So to avoid confrontation altogether, I've said I'm from Malta."

"But your surname isn't Egyptian," I noted.

Jonathan smiled sadly. "My father is British. He was in the army in Egypt when he met my mother. But him and me — we've never gotten along."

Jonathan proceeded to unfold the turbulent details of his life. Jonathan was the middle of three sons. His British father met his Coptic mother, Lydia, in Cairo. But the early part of their married life was spent in the East End of London, where Jonathan was born. However, with Lydia's pressing homesickness for Egypt, the father took his family back to Cairo, where he was employed as an electrical engineer.

Jonathan's memory of that first visit to Egypt was

one of soldiers and machine guns. The belligerency in the Middle East was a way of life, but most strange of all, in sharp contrast to the London church bells, were the mournful moanings of the muezzins calling the Moslems to prayer.

When he was 8 years old, Jonathan and his family moved to the Sudan. His father found a job in Khartoum for the Sudanese government, which was the Anglo-Egyptian Sudan at the time. They had moved there because Lydia had a sister married to a missionary in Khartoum. The country was in a state of unrest; in fact, that year, 1956, the Sudan received its independence from Britain. Jonathan could remember one day in Khartoum watching the statue of Gen. Charles Gordon being dismantled in a public square.

But Jonathan and his brothers didn't live in Khartoum with their parents. They were sent to an English-speaking Catholic school in Wad Medani on the Blue Nile about 100 miles away.

"I hadn't been there quite two years when I was expelled," Jonathan sighed. "I guess you could say I didn't have the right kind of upbringing. My parents were always arguing, and my father was a very hard man. I can remember the many times I stood between the two of them, trying to protect my mother, as my father came at her with saucepans. The priests and nuns that ran the school were strict beyond reason. My impression of Catholic Christianity in the Sudan was one of cruelty. One priest had an awful mode of punishment. He whipped the back of my legs with the tail of a rhinoceros. I thought I had suffered pain from my father's beatings, but this whipping hurt twice as much."

I winced as Jonathan continued his story: "After that incident, I was hurt and felt life had no meaning. Having no interest in my school work, I was expelled at the age of 10. I left my brothers at school and headed back to my parents. My father, pardon me for saying it, beat the hell out of me.

"I remember one day I asked my father, quite innocently, how to tie a knot. He couldn't be bothered. He told me to go away and leave him alone, or I'd get a hiding. I kept persisting for his attention. I got my hiding: a bad one. I was hit across the face with a shoe and for weeks I had a bruise mark on my face the shape of a plastic perforated sole. I was too embarrassed to go out of the house for two weeks.

"My father was always giving me the impression that I was the wasted son. This made me so angry that one day I set fire to two lemon trees in our back yard, and my father, to avenge the trees, tried to run me down in his jeep. I ran away until his anger died down.

"Meanwhile, my mother favoured my older brother. They called him the brainy one. The only affection I received was from a half dozen pigeons that we kept. They were white pigeons," Jonathan said, his voice halting. "They were like six precious angels to me."

When Jonathan was 13, the family moved back to England, and within the first week, his mother walked out on the family, never to be seen or heard of again.

"There I was, stuck with a father who hated my guts. Within one week of being back in London, I found myself behind bars. My father gave evidence in court that I was incorrigible. He lied and said I'd beaten my own mother black and blue — marks which, in actual fact, had always been caused by him.

"I was assigned to a detention home in Ealing, where the beatings came regularly, and I learned how to fight to survive among the other boys. I was later put in another home in Enfield where I didn't make my bed properly — nobody had given me instructions. Before I could ask questions, the fellow in charge punched me in the nose. Between the blood and tears, I still tried to find a smile."

Despite loneliness and repeated rejections, his smile was almost a constant facial fixture — not a mask, but a genuine warmth that could only have come from God's providence through the years. My own face, at this point, must have looked tortured. I was vicariously experiencing the injustice that had been dealt to this new brother of mine.

"I was determined to make it in life," Jonathan said to cheer me up. "With still no contact from my Mum, I was moved to another children's home in Teddington. Then, one day, I received a call from my father, who was now living with another woman in Brentwood. He said he wanted to make amends and invited me to live with them.

"Well, I didn't hold any grudge at the time. I guess I jumped at the attention. But soon the old patterns developed. The woman my father was living with already had sons of her own, particularly one named George, who was living at the house. George was given a key to the front door, but I was treated like a stepson. If I went out at night, I was expected to be home by 10:30, but I often had to wait outside until 1a.m. when George returned with the front door key.

"This lasted two months until one night I was out in the rain and cold, banging on the door, pleading for them to let me in. All of a sudden I could hear my father storming down the stairs. He opened the door and punched me in the nose. Out of my experience of fighting through two different children's homes, I was no coward. I accepted the punch, even though I was hurt, and proceeded straight up the stairs to bed. As I got to the top of the stairs, my father came at me again. I said to him, 'You've hit me once tonight, you'll never hit me again.' All I can remember was bundling down the stairs, the two of us, and he's a very heavy man. The next thing was my stepmother screaming at the top of her lungs: 'Get out! Get out!'

"I had no-one to turn to. I was in a strange town, turned out on the streets with only a bit of change in my pocket. I didn't know where my next meal was coming from. So my only hope was to do what a friend had already done — join the Merchant Navy. I was accepted and went to training school in Gloucester. Most of the fellows were also from broken homes. If you'll excuse the expression," he said jocularly, "all of us were in the same boat."

"My first vessel was a little cargo boat, the 'Beaver Oak,' owned by the Canadian Pacific Railway that sailed up the St. Lawrence River, and my first job was pantry boy. I was frightened by the 50-foot waves on my first Atlantic crossing. I was seasick all the time and lonely, but I had to keep on working. The other crew members were the 'hard as nails' variety. They didn't treat me like a friend, more like a border trade acquaintance — somebody you speak to only because you're stuck with 'em.

"After an assortment of voyages, I was told to join the shipping federation, and I was assigned to a ship that was carrying explosives to Vietnam. The night before I was to join ship, I had one last fling in a pub. I staggered after a London double decker bus, reached for the pole, and missed. I found myself sprawled in the street with my left arm broken. I missed the ship. But even then, the Lord was protecting me.

"Some months later, I was led to know that this particular ship was bombed from the air near Vietnam. I could have been one of the casualties!"

Jonathan was to have even more dramatic escapes from death at sea. But meanwhile, with his arm in a sling, he was unemployed. Through this turn of events, he met his wife-to-be, Ann, in a pub.

"I guess you could say, like me, she was drowning her sorrows. She already had two children, but because of my childhood, I felt sorry for them and took a liking to them."

Jonathan moved in with Ann, but the romance soon waned. She began to suspect he was a layabout.

"To prove myself, I went up to the shipping federation. My arm was now out of plaster, so they offered me a job for what appeared to be only three months. That would mean I'd be back for Christmas.

"I joined the ship as assistant steward in Casablanca. It was a 27,000-ton cargo tramp. I arrived in Casablanca thinking back on my days at Khartoum. The place held a certain magic for me. But there had been a misunderstanding over the articles of contract. I was very upset as I went up the gangway. Someone said: 'I hope you realise this is a two-year job, and we're off to Red China!'"

Dismayed that he wouldn't be home for Christmas, Jonathan sent telegrams and boxes of chocolates to Ann from various ports, but 'she didn't want to know'. He turned increasingly to alcohol for consolation as he was tossed to and fro on his berth on those lonely nights.

"Talk about a slow boat to China!" he grimaced. "After seven interminable weeks, the first port of call was Singapore. Shanghai was next on the itinerary. From there, we crossed the Pacific to the port of Prince Rupert in British Columbia, where we loaded grain to take back to China. Finally, in Canada, there was a letter waiting from Ann.

"Before receiving that letter, I didn't care if I lived or died. But then, two days out at sea, we hit a storm. It was early one morning, about 7.00. Me and the chief steward were looking out toward the forward end of the ship, talking about how rough it was. We learned later that it was a hurricane, and that five ships sunk, including a U.S. naval vessel.

"Suddenly, the chief steward grabbed hold of me and threw me down on the deck. There was an explosion of glass and wood. As I raised my head in the cold wind, I could see that the quarter-inch glass on the windows had been smashed right where we had been standing. The glass was dangling like long icicles, sharp as knives. I realised that again I had narrowly escaped death. If the chief steward hadn't thrown me down, I could have been dead because of the flying glass. Only a few days previous, I couldn't have cared less, but I had heard from Ann, and now I wanted desperately to live. Then I thought about the cargo of grain on board. If it got wet and swelled, we'd sink!

"Eventually, we limped into Shanghai with one gangway missing, not a railing left on the ship, half the bridge blown off, one lifeboat missing; every window and porthole on the forward was smashed, and the whole forward structure was dented inward from the heavy waves.

"The Chinese wouldn't entertain any ideas of repairs whatsoever. We had to unload, and from there, somehow make it to Japan for repairs. That took two months. I was still looking forward to getting back home to Ann, but that could be another year, if I survived that long on a ship that seemed to be cursed."

Japanese motor cars were loaded on the repaired ship for a faraway destination: Jacksonville, Florida. The captain never knew their next destination. He was always informed at the last minute by London. When Jonathan heard that the next call would be Spain, he made up his mind to jump ship.

"As it turned out, I was able to sign off in Spain.

Crewmen had been jumping ship left, right and centre all along. They couldn't take the hard life. From the time I got on until the time I left, 27 crewmen had jumped ship.

"In Spain they flew some of us back to London. I was in a panic to get a taxi. The first person I saw was Ann's oldest child, now my adopted daughter. She said one of the sweetest words I'd ever heard: Dad."

After Jonathan and Ann were married, one day he read a news account of a ship by the name of MV Howe Matton. It was the cargo ship that had taken him around the world. It had been off Pakistani waters where, at the time, there was a dispute with India. The ship had been accidentally torpedoed. Seven crewmen were killed. The torpedo crashed through the area of Jonathan's cabin where he'd lived for 12 months. If he had not signed off, he probably would be dead today.

After joining the QE2, once, during a Mediterranean cruise, Jonathan had searched in vain for his mother in Cairo. And, during the same cruise in Haifa, Israel, he had climbed Mount Carmel in search for God and a religious experience. But he returned to ship without any visible evidence of God. His misfortune reminded me of the prophet Hosea's words: "My people are destroyed for lack of knowledge." Jonathan, like so many confused seekers, did not know to look for answers in God's Word.

I was thrilled with the Lord's providential keeping power in Jonathan's life. However, the Holy Spirit impressed me that Jonathan had some forgiving to do before he could truly be set free. I asked him if he could forgive his father. His reply was hesitant: "I'll think about it."

☆ ☆ ☆

The next morning, Peter awakened early to photograph Diamond Head as the ship slipped away from Aloha Tower. Groggily, I told him about Jonathan and how he really wasn't from Malta but had Egyptian Coptic roots.

"That's a real honour," Peter said as he shaved.

I opened the porthole curtains and peeked out. The sunrise oranged the harbour. I continued to relate Jonathan's story to Peter and how Jonathan nursed a hatred for his Dad. The rockabye motion and the humming of the engines beckoned me to sleep in.

"No!" I said determinedly. "Time is short. We've got to go up to breakfast and talk to Jonathan about forgiving his father!"

Jonathan agreed to talk to us later that evening.

"But," he said, unconsciously making a fist as if his father had just walked into the restaurant, "you're touching a very sore spot."

☆ ☆ ☆

That evening Jonathan knocked at our cabin and asked if we would like to see how the other half lives.

We were delighted at the opportunity to visit the crew quarters. Down on Six Deck, the plush carpet disappeared in the hallways. But Jonathan's inside cabin seemed cosy and cheerful. On the walls were postcards from all over the world and a bedside lamp had been glued with coinage from many countries.

Jonathan wanted to know what the Scriptures teach about forgiveness. We noted the following principles:

— Jesus said our heavenly Father cannot forgive us if we're unable to forgive others (*Matthew 6:15*)
— The number of times we must forgive a person who has wronged us is 490 (70 times 7), or indefinitely,

according to *Matthew 18:22*

— Jesus Himself asked his Father to forgive his murderers (*Luke 23:34*)

— Forgiveness is unconditional, according to *Mark 11:25*,

'And whenever you stand praying, forgive, if you have anything against anyone; so that your Father also who is in heaven may forgive you your trespasses.'

— Unforgiveness can bind another person, according to *Matthew 18:18*, and forgiveness can also loose a person:

'Truly, I say to you, whatever you bind on earth shall be bound in heaven, and whatever you loose on earth shall be loosed in heaven.'

"I almost forgave my father once," Jonathan intoned. "I got all the way up to his front door, and then I turned away."

He sighed a big sigh: "But I see now if I've got to forgive, I've got to forgive! There's no way of getting round it."

It was a big step for him. Not accustomed to praying out loud, Jonathan's prayer was terse and to the point: "Lord, I ask for forgiveness for my father and all others who've ever done malice towards me."

Jonathan was beaming again as we left his cabin. But we had no sooner returned to our own cabin when he was at our door, this time carrying a box under his arm.

"I can't sleep with this thing in my cabin," he said, opening the box. It was a ouija board.

"Hallelujah! Let's throw it overboard," I exclaimed, lunging for the box.

"First," Peter said wisely, "I think we ought to pray with Jonathan about renouncing the occult." Peter as always was the perfect balance for my exuberance.

"We know that you've dabbled in the occult, Jonathan, and you said that your wife is from a family of fortunetellers. This power in your family is not from God," Peter continued, "and it must be broken so your household can be brought to Christ."

Jonathan was amazed to learn now clearly the Bible delineates forbidden occult practices from authentic guidance. His brown eyes widened as we showed him many passages in both the Old and New Testaments condemning all occult practices as abominations, including astrology, psychic mediums and consorting with familiar spirits. We explained that spirits at seances can actually be impersonating demons. They masquerade quite deliberately to deceive many with lying wonders. The most convincing passages were *Deuteronomy 18: 10−12‡, Isaiah 8:19†* and the account of King Saul consulting the witch of Endor and incurring God's anger.

The three of us held hands and bound the power of Satan in Jonathan's life in the Name of Jesus. Then we loosed him and his family from any past curses unto the Truth.

It was now midnight. We went up on the Port Deck with the ouija board. It was a momentous break with Jonathan's past.

"In the Name of Jesus, I renounce the occult," he shouted over the roar of the waves, and he tossed the seemingly innocent, but nevertheless accursed, board into the sea.

---

‡ There shall not be found among you any one who burns his son or his daughter as an offering, any one who practices divination, a soothsayer, or an augur, or a sorcerer, or a charmer, or a medium, or a wizard, or a necromancer. For whoever does these things is an abomination to the Lord. † And when they say to you: "Consult the mediums and the wizards who chirp and mutter," should not a people consult their God?

Chapter 12

Sean

'For false Christs and false
prophets will arise and show
great signs and wonders, so
as to lead astray,
if possible, even the elect.
(*Matthew 24: 24*)

Only two days remained before we were to disembark
in Los Angeles. The tide of my concern over Sean
O'Reily was rising with every knot that brought us
closer to the California shore. Inside me, the impression was even stronger that Sean had fallen into the trap
of a false cult. Every time I visited him in the Quarter
Deck Library, I had asked to peruse the literature of
the group he planned to join back in India.

He must have sensed himself that the group wasn't
'kosher'. Whenever I inquired about the literature, he
smacked his head absent-mindedly and muttered:
"Oh, I just can't remember to bring it to you. It's still
down in my cabin."

Then he'd suggest that I come back later. He kept
putting me off. This time, as I walked into the library,
he was finishing a letter to the group in Bombay.

"I've already sent them some money," he
volunteered, "and now I'm writing to say I've decided
to sell my house and join them just as soon as I can
terminate my duties on this ship."

He pushed the letter aside and thrust some pamphlets

into my hand. "Here. I remembered to bring these before you disembark."

At last. But my heart quickly sank. It was the propaganda of a prominent false cult. The name of the organisation was plainly in view. There was no getting around it — in his loneliness and need for love, John was entangled in a spider's web.

Clutching the pamphlets, I wondered what to say. I decided to go to the cabin and ask the Lord to unmask the deception. Meanwhile, Sean's sudden determination to abandon all increased the urgency of the situation.

I sat down on my berth and sifted through the pamphlets. It didn't take long to see through the veneer of the religious rhetoric: salvation was not through Jesus Christ; the Bible was not authoritative.

Peter popped into the cabin, said he'd been looking for me. Silently, I handed him the booklets. His face fell.

"How is it possible," I asked, "that somebody like Sean O'Reily, who has been grounded in the faith all his life, could suddenly be sucked into a cult?"

The subtlety of counterfeit Christianity angered me. I pondered: if Sean O'Reily, a member of the Salvation Army, can be spiritually hoodwinked, then what hope is there for the less informed sheep?

For a long while I interceded for him with tears. Then, suddenly catching a glimpse of myself in the mirror, I realised my eyes were bloodshot. With a sigh, I washed my face and headed for the upper decks through the Midships Lobby. Of all people, Sean O'Reily was passing through the lobby at that moment with a load of books on a trolley.

"What's the matter? You've been crying."

"Sean, our time left on board is short, so I'm not going to mince words. I've just read that literature." I steeled myself for a possible confrontation. "It has upset me very much, and I've been praying for you." I paused. "I'm sure you know the Bible warns us that even in the last days the elect will be deceived, if it were possible. This group of yours is a cult, and I'm terribly worried about you."

I thought his Irish temper might flare, and I expected him to launch a defence of the group. Instead, he patted me on the arm and said reassuringly: "I'll talk to you about it some more before Los Angeles. I promise."

He didn't sleep that night. Seeing me 'by chance' and my red eyes had shaken him. Several times during the night he considered calling our cabin, but he backed down when he picked up the phone. The next morning, our last full day on the QE2, Sean was summoned before the staff captain.

"Well, of all people, I never expected to see you here on a charge." The staff captain's words hit Sean like fiery darts.

A passenger had written a nasty letter of complaint, accusing Sean of deliberately shortchanging his wife of 40 pence when she purchased some stamps in the Quarter Deck Library.

Sean defended himself by explaining the difficult stamp procedure. It involved converting various passengers' currencies into the right amount to pay for stamps of still different nationalities at each port. Confusion always mounted as disgruntled passengers became impatient in the stamp queue.

Nevertheless, he was advised to plead guilty. Unfortunately, if he pleaded 'not guilty' the passenger didn't plan to let the matter die. So Sean was reprimanded for a petty crime he did not consciously commit. This was a blow to his integrity.

Feeling dejected, Sean sought out Peter for some brotherly consolation. They went to our cabin to talk.

When I dashed into the cabin before lunch, I was surprised by the closeness of the air. It was as if wrestling had been going on — spiritual wrestling, I was soon to learn. Perspiration still lined Sean's forehead. He truly looked wrung out.

He had shared the stamp incident with Peter. He felt guilty before the Lord for having lied just to quell a confrontation, and, most of all, he was wounded by the injustice.

Peter reminded him of the injustice that even Jesus was meted at the hands of a tribunal. Then Peter had carefully reviewed the cultic literature with Sean, pointing out the fallacies according to the Bible, and miraculously, Sean had been able to see through the maze of deception!

"Tell you what we'll do," Sean said to me with a burst of enthusiasm. "Let's just throw this away."

He tore the literature into pieces and tossed them into the bin. "Let's pray," Sean said, clasping our hands and unashamedly falling to his knees. Obviously, he felt no qualms about praying out loud. He was joyous as he renounced the cult.

"Lord, I know these people are my true brother and sister. Hear their prayers, Lord. Always hear their prayers." Then he stood up and embraced Peter and kissed my hand.

With less than 24 hours remaining on board for us, Sean was delivered from the false cult! God's timing is never a day too late.

☆　☆　☆

Sean O'Reily was the last person to whom we said farewell on a gray day when the QE2 docked in Los Angeles. We exchanged addresses, and he gave us a photo of himself in his Salvation Army uniform. On

116

the back, he inscribed: 'God's love is wonderful.'

Then he told us some good news. After the confrontation the previous day with the staff captain, another letter had been delivered to the captain in the late afternoon. This time it was a letter praising Sean. Some passenger had seen Sean being harangued in the library by the disgruntled woman whose husband wrote the nasty letter. This passenger had been so impressed by Sean's courtesy under the verbal abuse that she wrote the staff captain to compliment the QE2 for such a mannerly crew member!

"So," Sean said victoriously, "the slate has been wiped clean."

He was vindicated. It was as if God's protection had been temporarily withdrawn as long as Sean was dabbling with the cult. But as soon as he was back under the protection and will of God, having renounced the cult, the other letter came 'out of the blue'.

Epilogue

"Welcome QE2 from Queen Mary crew members."

The message was hand-lettered on a bed sheet and suspended on a pleasure boat in the San Pedro channel.

California was the new home for Cunard's old luxury liner and the QE2's ancestor. In the harbour area of Long Beach, the Queen Mary was permanently harnessed to the pier, her sea-going capacity now gutted to accommodate a convention hotel and a 'Living Sea Museum'.

It was a windy and overcast day as the ship moved into the harbour among oil derricks and working cranes. Peter and I sadly abandoned the observation deck for one final breakfast. My only consolation was that I had actually lost weight during the cruise even though I hardly ever missed one of the six meals a day, including the midnight buffet. (The only 'meal' I skipped was 'elevens', but I still managed to lose half a stone because of daily exercise in the gym, refusing dinner rolls and ordering grapefruits in lieu of desserts. It's a great diet.)

But for our final breakfast, Peter jokingly ordered the entire menu. Charlie was quick to respond with his own last laugh. He laid an empty plate in front of Peter and tore the menu card into little bite-sized pieces.

"There you are, sir. The entire menu."

Peter's expression was priceless.

"Do you require catsup, sir?" Charlie inquired in his most polite British manner. He poured a dollop of tomato sauce onto the shredded menu. Jay, Tiffany and Jonathan roared with laughter as the gag developed.

119

After finishing a real breakfast, we rose reluctantly to say farewell. Oliver had disappeared into the kitchen, saying he hated goodbyes. Jonathan knew him well enough to realise that Oliver felt a little sentimental about our leaving, and so he fetched Oliver for an endearing round of hugs, photos and solemn promises from all to write.

It wasn't quite so difficult saying farewell to our jet-setting friends, Jay and Tiffany, because we'd already made plans to visit them in Toronto. We had a grand re-union. Tiffany requested prayers for her family, and Jay introduced me to Yonge Street, the most sordid area, where he adventurously suggested that I should hand out tracts. He apparently was still fascinated with anybody who would dare to do such a thing. I obliged by giving salvation tracts to people in the doors of video shops while he took snapshots of me in action with his own camera. (In his spirit, Jay longs to do the same thing; he just doesn't know it yet. But God's hand is upon him.)

☆   ☆   ☆

As we descended the QE2's gangway for the last time, I felt a hollow aching like a mother abandoning her children. All we could do now was pray for our new brothers on board to be nurtured by the Lord.

Two weeks later, when the QE2 docked in New York, we received a long distance call from Jonathan. He said he had been crying like a baby — the first time he'd been able to cry in years.

"Do you remember that night when you asked me to forgive my father?" His voice was still shaky.

"Of course, we do."

"Well, I received word today that my father is dead. I figured out the date, and he died the night that

I forgave him!"

His father had been in hospital with a kidney ailment. His life hung in limbo for weeks. But the Lord graciously did not allow him to die without first giving Jonathan the opportunity — and the peace of mind — of releasing him through forgiveness.

"I'm just amazed at God's timing," Jonathan said. "I'm so glad God gave me the strength to forgive him when I did."

Then, several days later, we received a post card from Jonathan. That one card alone was worth the price of the cruise. It was a thank you message that he had selected from Matthew 10:42,

'And whoever gives to one of these
little ones even a cup of cold water
because he is a disciple, truly, I
say to you, he shall not lose his reward.'